ALIGNING YOUR PLANETS

ALIGNING YOUR PLANETS

An Astrological Journal for
Self-Reflection, Growth, and Balance

Alice Sparkly Kat

CHRONICLE PRISM

Contents

Astrology Supports Your Survival | 7

Astrology Supports Your Survival

THERE'S THE CANON OF ASTROLOGY, with its textbooks and delineations (descriptions of astrological placements, transits, predictions, or aspects) and proverbs, but there's also the "fanon" of astrology—where people make astrological meaning by flirting with each other, by remediating experiences through their own rituals, and by writing cyclical stories until they believe in themselves. Client work, because it is about playing and talking with other people, resides in the fanon part of astrology. It is about caring about people. The people who practice client work as astrologers tend to come from the retail world, hospitality industries, sex work, and social work.

When I began my client practice in 2015, the work was about gathering. People would come with their friends and we would have long conversations about their lives and charts together. This was when my practice was much more local. The people who came to me were all from the area I lived in. We would go into my bedroom, where a bookshelf created an area separate from my sleeping quarters for client work. I didn't really have space to host people, and people who knew my roommates would stop in to say hello mid-session. Many times, my roommates and clients were in community.

Over time, my client practice has grown to accommodate more people from beyond New York. My practice has also become more somatic as it has become more virtual. As my own relationship to the body and the spirit changed, I acquired more tools. My trauma, pain, and grief literacy comes from the schools of Morita therapy, focusing, parts work, and Chinese body work. My practice is always evolving. I have always believed that it is important to remain intellectually promiscuous. You should never believe in one thing completely and you should also know and welcome the contradictions that it takes to really think about things. I remind myself that pleasure and play work to heal, and that prophecy works to heal. I also understand that not everyone processes emotions in the same way, that feelings aren't universal, and that there will be people who find this workbook useful and people who do not.

The material in this journal has transformed since my relationship to astrology has changed, but the goal behind it has remained the same: Use this book to advocate for your essential right to safety—safety in your body, in love, in sex, in language, and in relationship—and to feel absolutely livid when you are denied safety. Understand that when a person is denied safety, it is not an individual failing but a sign of societal and ethical failure. Notice the physical, social, financial, and spiritual wounds of suffering. Never negate suffering's impact, and build the imagination to live. Remember that you don't know what will happen in the future: There are always more futures than the ones that seem the most available. When one future is taken away, when one survival strategy falters, you can always create or remember another.

There are as many astrologies as there are astrologers. There is also no one right way to use astrology. What astrology tries to serve is your own feeling of aliveness.

This journal should be used with intellectual promiscuity in mind. You do not need to believe in astrology to use this book. Work through some chapters halfheartedly and others wholeheartedly. There is no particular order in which you need to answer the prompts here. Feel free to use them in order, out of order, on the transits and astrological events that they are made for, or anytime in between. You can use the Jupiter return worksheet when Jupiter enters the sign that your natal Jupiter is in or when it has already drifted away, in processing how your imagination shifted and continues to shift. Space is provided in this journal for you to write whatever you need. You can use the book to jump off into further discussions in a more traditional, blank journal. You can use a prompt within this book as resistance if you feel yourself angered or upset by what it evokes, or refuse the prompt altogether. Explore with curiosity what this resistance means to you and why it is important to you.

Aligning Your Planets comes out of the years of client work that I have behind me so far. It reflects how I work with people on different cycles and celestial events. It's not the only way to think about a Mercury retrograde or a Saturn return. Please use the book in a way that works for you. I hope that you leave it worn, colored on, drawn on, and written in. This is your journal. Your responses to the journal are yours alone.

SOLAR RETURN

FREQUENCY	SIGNIFICANCE	WHEN IT HAPPENS
Occurs every year on your birthday	Power, aliveness, childlikeness, celebration, pride	For the entirety of the day when the Sun returns to the degree of your natal Sun

YOUR SOLAR RETURN IS WHEN the transiting Sun returns to where it was when you were born. It's your birthday!

Too much of the time, we expect ourselves to perform joy on our birthdays for the benefit of another's gaze. We spend our time curating parties, worrying over which of our friends might not like each other, and wondering whether we are not having fun if we don't stay out past a certain hour. But this is your fucking birthday. This is about celebrating the want over the should. Birthdays are about believing enough in your desire that you know with certainty that, with just a little attention, it will become a future.

There's no one way to celebrate a birthday. There's no reason not to celebrate it with a nap, an orgasm, alone, with fifty people, or with just one friend, and there's no reason not to celebrate it by spending no money at all. The birthday celebration is a ritual that you are allowed to design in any way that you want. Cut a cord, book a photoshoot, or repot a plant.

Last Year Was
a Journey

A solar return is just like any planet's return. It finishes one cycle while starting a new one. On our birthday, we remember who we were at our last birthday. We bring that emotional body with us.

Let's do something fun and rewrite your last year into the narrative of a hero's journey.

Every hero's journey has an antagonist. That could be people, institutions, abstract feelings, or another force. What were your main challenges?

_____

_____

_____

_____

_____

_____

_____

What decisions did you make?

_____

_____

_____

_____

_____

An important part of a hero's journey is the threshold—the point at which you realize what your mission is. Mentors and helpers, such as friends, can help you at this point. When did you realize what you wanted? Who helped you realize this?

_____

_____

_____

_____

Every hero has temptations. What were your strongest temptations?

_____

_____

_____

_____

The climax of a hero's development is the death and rebirth revelation—when the hero realizes what all their sacrifices have been for. What was your death and rebirth revelation? How did your goals change?

_____

_____

_____

_____

After the revelation, the hero returns home, but not without a period of atonement. At this point in the story, the hero leaves parts of their old self behind and becomes something new. What did you have to leave behind in order to return?

_____

_____

_____

_____

Birthday Wishes

Use this solar return guide to make some wishes for your next year. In each box, write down some things that you'd like to do in that month.

DURING THE MONTH
OF YOUR BIRTHDAY
———
What rituals do you use to celebrate
your continued life?

ONE MONTH AFTER
YOUR BIRTHDAY
———
How do you support the
intentions of those celebration rituals
from last month?

TWO MONTHS AFTER
YOUR BIRTHDAY
———
How do you support curiosity
and change?

THREE MONTHS AFTER
YOUR BIRTHDAY
———
How do you protect your expectations
of safety and privacy?

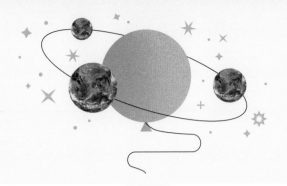

FOUR MONTHS AFTER
YOUR BIRTHDAY
———
How are you going to play?

FIVE MONTHS AFTER
YOUR BIRTHDAY
———
What burdens have you taken on?
Do you agree with your reasons for
taking on those burdens?

SIX MONTHS AFTER
YOUR BIRTHDAY
———
How amenable are you to support?
What makes you shy away
from support?

SEVEN MONTHS AFTER
YOUR BIRTHDAY
———
What do you feel like you owe other
people? Do you agree with your debts?

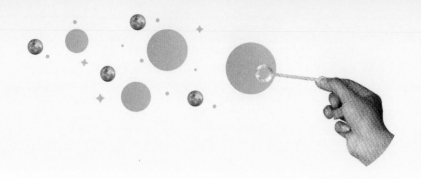

EIGHT MONTHS AFTER YOUR BIRTHDAY

What types of vastness are easily available to you? What types of vastness are harder to access?

NINE MONTHS AFTER YOUR BIRTHDAY

How has your expectation of the world changed since your last birthday?

TEN MONTHS AFTER YOUR BIRTHDAY

What makes you and your community wiser?

ELEVEN MONTHS AFTER YOUR BIRTHDAY

How can you advocate for your right to rest?

ADDITIONAL NOTES:

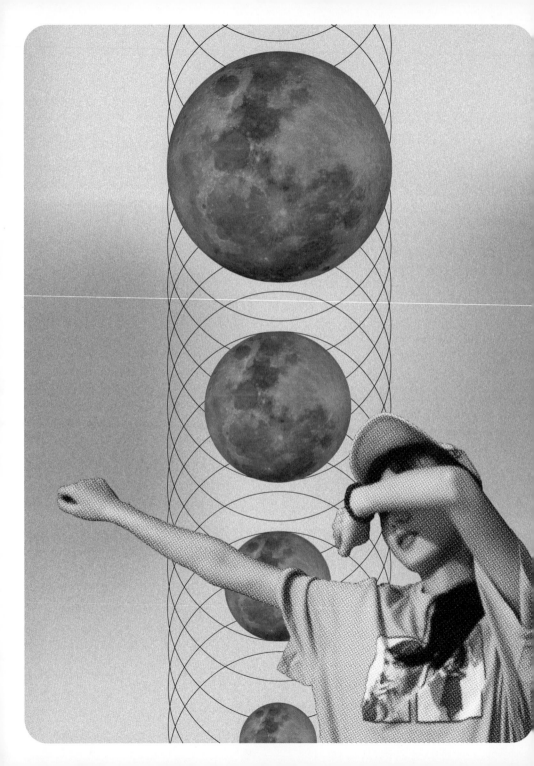

NEW MOON

FREQUENCY	SIGNIFICANCE	WHEN IT HAPPENS
Occurs every 29 to 30 days, usually once in every Gregorian calendar month	Sleep, rest, exhaustion, menstruation, whimsy	When the Moon conjoins with the Sun

NEW MOONS ARE NOT FOR DOING NEW THINGS. A lot of us are tired during New Moons! Being and feeling tired is one of your body's most important strategies for showing you what you do not want anymore. Here is a removal exercise and dream journal to help support your tiredness.

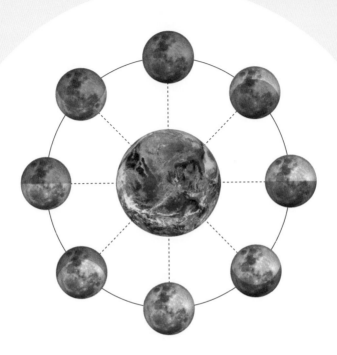

REMOVAL RITUAL

Note: This ritual uses fire. Please practice caution if you do this ritual by keeping body parts, including hands, away from burning flames and using a fireproof bowl. Do not use plastic or wood. Consider doing this ritual outdoors on a non-windy day.

Perform this removal exercise in a quiet space where you are comfortable. You will need paper, a pencil or pen, a bowl, water, and a lighter or matches.

ONE

Find a small fireproof bowl. Ceramic, metal, or glass will do.
If you are new to working with fire, consider adding water to the bowl.

TWO

Find a piece of paper and something to write with.

THREE

Take five minutes to reflect on your month, all the things that happened,
and remember how you felt about those events.

FOUR

Pick two or three experiences that keep you up at night,
to get rid of for the next cycle.

FIVE

Write those thoughts on the piece of paper.

SIX

Inhale; then, as you exhale, burn the piece of paper over your bowl.

SEVEN

Drop the burning paper into the bowl.

EIGHT

If you want, jump over the fire in the bowl so that you don't
carry your luck with you. Be careful that you don't knock over the bowl
or catch your pants on fire when you do this! You can wait until the
burning paper in the bowl is smoldering when doing this step or
you can choose not to do it at all if fire freaks you out.

Dream Log

NOTES FROM MY DREAM

Date: _____

Symbols: _____

_____

_____

Connections to waking life: _____

_____

_____

_____

_____

_____

NOTES FROM MY DREAM

Date: _____

Symbols: _____

_____

Tarot pull in the morning: _____

_____

_____

_____

_____

_____

NOTES FROM MY DREAM

Date: _____

Symbols: _____

_____

_____

Astrological transits that night: _____

_____

_____

_____

_____

_____

_____

_____

NOTES FROM MY DREAM

Date: _____

Symbols: _____

_____

_____

Connections to movies/books I'm watching/reading: _____

_____

_____

_____

_____

_____

_____

_____

NOTES FROM MY DREAM

Date: _____

Symbols: _____

_____

_____

What I ate the night before: _____

_____

_____

_____

_____

_____

_____

NOTES FROM MY DREAM

Date: _____

Symbols: _____

_____

_____

Connections to other dreams I've had: _____

_____

_____

_____

_____

_____

_____

_____

NOTES FROM MY DREAM

Date: _____

Symbols: _____

_____

_____

What _____ said when I told them about my dream: _____

_____

_____

_____

_____

_____

_____

_____

NOTES FROM MY DREAM

Date: _____

Symbols: _____

_____

What I thought about before falling asleep: _____

_____

_____

_____

_____

_____

ADDITIONAL NOTES:

FULL
MOON

FREQUENCY	SIGNIFICANCE	WHEN IT HAPPENS
Occurs every 29 to 30 days, usually once in every Gregorian calendar month	Eating, pooping, metabolizing, menstruating, direction	When the Moon opposes the Sun or is 180 degrees away

THE FULL MOON HAPPENS when the Moon opposes or is 180 degrees away from the Sun. The Full Moon will always be in a sign that is opposite of the solar season. Physically, we tend to become more active during a Full Moon. Noticing where we feel full inside is one of our body's most important strategies for letting us know what we already have.

Consumption Log

There is a lot of pleasure in swallowing—that is, from consumption. But it is hard as hell to feel safe in consumption. We are urged to consume yet punished for needing to eat, needing clothes, and sometimes even for needing help. We are also taught, with terrifying precision, how to make ourselves more consumable and more palatable. For many of us, it somehow feels safer to be swallowed than to do the swallowing.

Write about your consumption. Do it seriously and empathetically—something that is hard to do. Write about food and also about fictions, imaginaries, and stories. Write about culture and all of the things that nourish you.

This past month, I have consumed:

SOMETHING DEAD:

SOMETHING WHOLE:

SOMETHING SWEET:

SOMETHING HARD:

SOMETHING SOUR:

SOMETHING TOXIC:

SOMETHING BITTER:

SOMETHING YUMMY:

SOMETHING SALTY:

SOMETHING BRANDED:

SOMETHING BLAND:

SOMETHING SPICY:

SOMETHING NECESSARY:

SOMETHING DELICIOUS:

Celebrate your appetite. Complete the following statements until you are satisfied:

MY APPETITE is my hunger for life.

MY APPETITE keeps me alive.

MY APPETITE works alongside my curiosity and my creativity.

MY APPETITE makes me a troublemaker.

MY APPETITE laughs when I try to tell it what to want.

MY APPETITE sits smug when it is satisfied.

MY APPETITE _____

_____

MY APPETITE _____

_____

MY APPETITE _____

_____

MY APPETITE _____

_____

MY APPETITE _____

_____

MY APPETITE _____

_____

MY APPETITE _____

_____

MY APPETITE _____

_____

MY APPETITE _____

_____

ECLIPSE SEASON

FREQUENCY	SIGNIFICANCE	WHEN IT HAPPENS
Occurs two times a year	Removal, being fed up, needing more, yearning	When the Sun is in the same signs as either of the two lunar nodes

ECLIPSES HAPPEN WHEN THE MOON, Earth, and Sun line up in a particular way. At these times, the Earth either blocks the light projected from the Sun to the Moon or the Moon blocks the light projected from the Sun to the Earth. Eclipses happen when the Sun transits close to the lunar nodes, which are the points in which the Moon moves into the Northern or Southern Hemispheres.

Imagine an eclipse as a great big pair of scissors that cuts things in half. Eclipses cut the edges of things off so that only a center remains. This removal is important and necessary. There is as much satisfaction and expression in removal and refusal as there is in gain.

Not every eclipse is significant to you. Eclipses happen several times a year. Of greater significance to you are the eclipses that happen when you are around 18 years old, around 36 years old, around 54 years old, around 72 years old, and around 90 years old. In fact, because the nodes of the Moon can cause drastic changes, you may feel as though you are living a different life once you have passed through the eclipse's portal.

Saying No

Saying no takes a lot of power. One reason for that is we are not able to control the choices available to us. Sometimes, our ability to say no to something can come from a place of privilege, such as the ability to say no to a job without fearing poverty. Or, we may feel as though we do not have the ability to say no to doing a favor for a parent without worrying that the parent will make a bureaucratic mistake. Often, we feel guilty about saying no to those who can afford our refusal rather than to those who do not yet have access to the choices that we have. This discrepancy is because capital tends to construct debt in terms that support power instead of deconstructing it.

The next time you face something you want to say no to and have time to think about it, complete this exercise first.

What emotions show up in your body when you imagine yourself saying no? Circle any that apply or fill in an emotion in your own words.

Achievement	Freedom	Regret
Anger	Frustration	Relief
Anxiety	Guilt	Sadness
Appreciation	Hotheadedness	Safety
Brightness	Humility	Satisfaction
Calm	Indebtedness	Terror
Disconnection	Joy	Tiredness
Doubt	Nausea	_____
Fear	Pride	_____
Firmness	Protection	_____

ARE YOU ABLE TO GIVE CONSENT,
or would your yes be assumed by someone? What would be some reasons for your yes?

WOULD YOU BE SUPPORTED IN YOUR NO?

In what ways? And in what ways might you lack support for your no?

WHAT WOULD HAPPEN IF YOU SAID NO?

Are you coming to this choice with a sense of agency, or of deprivation or frustration?
What needs to change before you are able to afford your no?

When we are not able to refuse, even though we need to for our own integrity, we do not stop wishing we could. Sometimes, we end up blaming ourselves for that wish. We start to wish that we could just say yes without drama and without emotions. We start to normalize our lack of consent. When a denied no causes suffering, it is important to stay with this suffering. This suffering is part of the truth of your experience. Even when we are unable to refuse what we want to refuse, our nos can bring us toward possibility.

Considering what needs to change before you are able to afford your no, explore a bit deeper.

What kind of world would make your refusal possible?

_____

_____

_____

_____

_____

_____

How would you behave if you knew without a doubt that this world were possible tomorrow?

_____

_____

_____

_____

_____

_____

What are some ways that you can celebrate a world that is not yet possible but could become possible?

_____

_____

_____

_____

_____

What might your consent heal?

_____

_____

_____

_____

Who benefits from your refusal?

_____

_____

_____

_____

How can you celebrate your ability to choose regardless of how you choose?

_____

_____

_____

_____

_____

A CELEBRATION
OF CONSENT

Giving yourself a hug

✧

Telling a friend about your choice

✧

Supporting the nos of those who can't yet afford the refusal that you can,
by asking them what they might need to say no

✧

Declaring your refusal in situations where other people can celebrate it

✧

Accepting compliments for your refusal

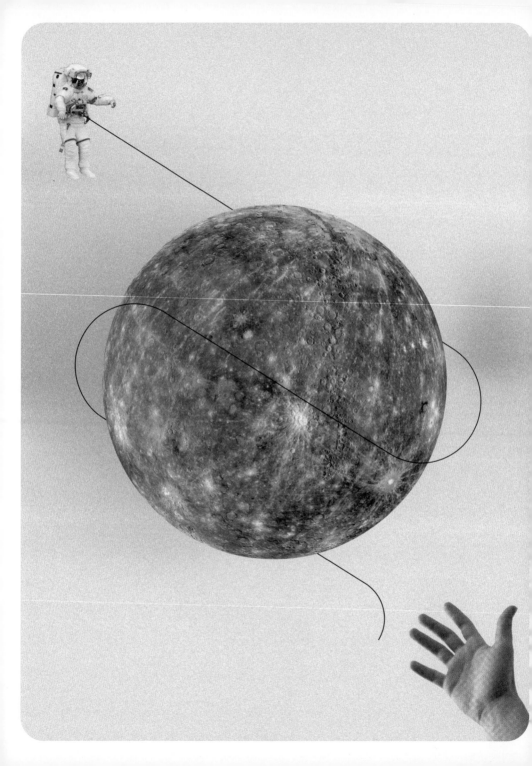

MERCURY RETROGRADE

FREQUENCY	SIGNIFICANCE	WHEN IT HAPPENS
Occurs around three times a year	Rest, pause, slowness, redo, learning	When Mercury is at its maximum elongation from the Sun as an evening star

MERCURY'S RETROGRADES AREN'T JUST WHEN communication supposedly breaks down—it's when our expectations around labor break open. It's when our hard drives erase themselves, when we need extra time for assignments and projects, and when we try to go one place but end up somewhere else entirely.

Mercury's retrograde happens the way it does because it is an "inferior" planet, meaning that it is closer to the Sun than the Earth. Unlike the "superior" planets, which retrograde where they oppose the Sun from the Earth's vantage point about once a year, Mercury retrogrades around three times a year. When Mercury is not retrograde, it is often recovering from its retrograde or preparing to retrograde.

When Mercury retrogrades, it will move past the Sun in an inferior conjunction. This point of Mercury's retrograde is important, as is the point where it stops its apparent motion and, again, appears to stand still in the sky. Mercury stops when it's at another maximum elongation from the Sun.

Overexplaining

It took me a long time to realize that explaining does not always lead to understanding or empathy. And I used to explain things a lot! I used to over-explain to my parents, roommates, community, partners, white bosses, and male clients, among others.

A lot of this overexplaining happened in my head. When you feel invalidated or misunderstood, you start to believe that everything requires an explanation, and you end up constantly overexplaining yourself to an imaginary person in your head rather than an actual person in the world.

There is nothing wrong with wanting social validation! We need it. But you shouldn't allow the absolute joy of validation to fall into the control of someone who has never been willing to see you. Or to be dictated by a concept of community that insists on minimizing your emotions. Minimizing your emotions is a survival skill that you don't need anymore.

Overexplaining your lived reality to a critic inside your head is just another manifestation of anxiety. Anxiety is often camouflaged; when we are scared all the time, it is hard to recognize. Anxiety may disguise itself as attachment, as righteousness, or even as care. When it disguises itself as connection, we become very dependent on how another person perceives our identity—we need them to validate our identity in order for us to believe in it ourselves.

The difference between explaining yourself to a real person—because you trust that you will be heard—and overexplaining yourself to an imagined idea of a person is just that: It is the difference between real and imagined relationships. Overexplaining yourself to imaginary people can take the form of loop-like thinking, of diatribes, of emotional flip-flopping, and of doubt, doubt, and more doubt. Overexplaining often happens in your head or on the internet.

MERCURY RETROGRADE

45

When you explain things to real people, you're engaging in a real conversation with emotional honesty. When you overexplain yourself to imaginary people, you are trying to protect yourself with excuses for being the way that you are, because you believe that you will not be met with empathy.

Some imaginary people who we might feel a need to overexplain things to:
- Children
- Colleagues
- Community
- Exes
- Parents
- Roommates
- Strangers
- Supervisors
- Therapists

Things that we might feel like we need to overexplain:
- Why we didn't text back by a certain time
- Why we are late
- Why we're angry
- What our gender is
- Why we dress the way we do
- Why we date who we date
- Why we experience pain

What overexplaining looks like:
- Ruminating all day on why you did or didn't do something with an imaginary captive audience in mind, but not saying anything to anyone in real life about it
- Writing an essay explaining your experience to an internet stranger who has never met you and responds to you with hostility
- Launching into self-deprecating explanations when someone gives you a compliment
- Trying to teach your parents how to parent
- Giving evidence that the harm you experienced was harmful by citing historical examples or statistics without centering your own reality
- Becoming an expert on your own trauma in languages that are accessible for authority figures

What are five things that you have overexplained before?

ONE

TWO

THREE

FOUR

FIVE

For everything that you have felt the need to overexplain over the years, finish the following sentences:

I OVEREXPLAINED because I felt angry that my needs were erased.

I OVEREXPLAINED because my experiences of assault were different from the stereotypical definitions.

I OVEREXPLAINED because I was taught that I exist to meet other people's needs.

I OVEREXPLAINED _____

_____

I OVEREXPLAINED _____

_____

I OVEREXPLAINED _____

_____

I OVEREXPLAINED _____

_____

I OVEREXPLAINED _____

_____

I OVEREXPLAINED _____

_____

I OVEREXPLAINED _____

_____

I OVEREXPLAINED _____

_____

I OVEREXPLAINED _____

_____

I OVEREXPLAINED _____

_____

Write about an empathetic encounter—an experience when you were met with empathy for something that you'd had a lot of anxiety about. What made you feel safe enough to share your experience? Sometimes we say things we hadn't planned to, and that can be a good thing. Identify something you discovered about yourself in that experience—something you would not have learned if you had planned everything out ahead of time.

Conflict Mapping

Here is a simple conflict mapping synastry activity. Synastry is the practice of relating two people's birth charts together. Conflict mapping is about describing a conflict so that it becomes clear to you. When we are engaged in conflict, the conflict itself is often unclear because we identify with our emotions around the conflict. Invite the person who you are in conflict with to do this exercise with you.

LOOK AT YOUR OWN MOON

What sign is your Moon in? What house?

How do you experience your Moon?

What childhood experiences do you associate with your Moon?

How have you emotionally matured as you became an adult?

LOOK AT WHAT ASPECTS YOUR MOON MAKES TO YOUR MARS

What sign and house is your Mars in?

Does your Moon make an aspect (conjunction, opposition, square, sextile, trine) to your Mars?

If so, what might this tell you about how you express emotions?

If not, what might this tell you about difficulties you may have in expressing emotions?

LOOK AT WHAT ASPECTS YOUR MOON MAKES TO YOUR VENUS

What sign and house is your Venus in?

Does your Moon make an aspect (conjunction, opposition, square, sextile, trine) to your Venus?

If so, what might this tell you about how you hold emotions?

If not, what might this tell you about difficulties you may have in holding emotions?

LOOK AT THE OTHER PERSON'S MOON

What sign is their Moon in? What house?

How do you experience this person's Moon, while keeping in mind that this is different from their experience of their own Moon?

What aspects does their Moon make with your Moon? Do they square, conjunct, or oppose each other? Do they sextile or trine?

**LOOK AT WHAT ASPECTS THE OTHER PERSON'S MOON
MAKES TO THEIR MARS**

What sign and house is their Mars in?

Does their Moon make an aspect (conjunction,
opposition, square, sextile, trine) to their Mars?

If so, what might this tell you about how this person expresses emotions?

If not, what might this tell you about difficulties that
this other person may have in expressing emotions?

**LOOK AT WHAT ASPECTS THE OTHER PERSON'S MOON
MAKES TO THEIR VENUS**

What sign and house is their Venus in?

Does their Moon make an aspect (conjunction,
opposition, square, sextile, trine) to their Venus?

If so, what might this tell you about how this person holds emotions?

If not, what might this tell you about difficulties that this other person
may have in holding emotions?

LOOK AT WHAT ASPECTS THE OTHER PERSON'S MOON MAKES TO YOUR MARS

Does their Moon make an aspect (conjunction, opposition, square, sextile, trine) to your Mars?

What might this tell you about how they respond to the ways that you express emotions?

LOOK AT WHAT ASPECTS THE OTHER PERSON'S MOON MAKES TO YOUR VENUS

Does their Moon make an aspect (conjunction, opposition, square, sextile, trine) to your Venus?

What might this tell you about how they respond to the ways that you hold on to emotions?

**LOOK AT WHAT ASPECTS YOUR MOON MAKES
TO THE OTHER PERSON'S MARS**

Does your Moon make an aspect (conjunction,
opposition, square, sextile, trine) to their Mars?

What might this tell you about how you respond to
the ways that they express emotions?

**LOOK AT WHAT ASPECTS YOUR MOON MAKES
TO THE OTHER PERSON'S VENUS**

Does your Moon make an aspect (conjunction,
opposition, square, sextile, trine) to their Venus?

What might this tell you about how you respond to
the ways that you hold on to emotions?

What are three things that the two of you learned from doing this activity that you would like to talk about together?

1. _____

_____

_____

2. _____

_____

_____

3. _____

_____

_____

What are some things that you need to see happen for the relationship to be repaired? What are some things that the other person needs to see happen before the relationship is repaired? Are there any nonnegotiables? Conflicts between your needs? Compromises you are both willing to make?

_____

_____

_____

_____

_____

_____

_____

_____

_____

_____

_____

VENUS
RETROGRADE

FREQUENCY	SIGNIFICANCE	WHEN IT HAPPENS
Occurs every two years	Hermit, hiding, forced interaction, cleaning, boundaries	When Venus is at its maximum elongation from the Sun as an evening star

VENUS RETROGRADES HAPPEN EVERY 584 DAYS. Venus's solar phase cycle is extremely regular, with Venus retrograding in the same sign every eight years. This means that the relative position of the Earth, the Sun, and Venus repeats every eight years. When this cycle is mapped out, Venus's cycle looks like a pentagram or a flower with five petals.

Like Mercury, Venus is an inferior planet that is closer to the Sun than the Earth. As a planet, Venus is about protection and withholding. If Venus retrograde is a time when protection goes awry, then it is also a time for doubting beauty, doubting gender, and doubting borders.

Venus is about love, sex, and pleasure. For many of us, these are things that can feel dangerously unsafe. There is love that protects innocence, and there is love that assumes no innocence. It is possible to believe in love while doubting beauty, while doubting gender, and while doubting innocence. It is possible to risk love and find unexpected safety, even when our most jaded and tired selves depend on our fear.

"Beauty is not a state of being seen but a state of being. Beauty can only arise in situations of deep self-trust and self-compassion."

Beauty

What do you actually mean when you use the words *attractive* or *beautiful*?
Pick two or three words from this list that jump out at you or stir an emotional
response, or add your own.

Accepted	Honest	Sensual
Accountable	Intuitive	Shiny
Alive	Loved	Smart
Blessed	Loving	Soft
Colorful	Memorable	Spiritual
Compassionate	Mysterious	Stable
Cool	Old	Sturdy
Creative	Open	Successful
Cute	Passionate	Understood
Deep	Popular	Wanted
Desired	Powerful	Warm
Devoted	Precious	Well rested
Dreamy	Protected	Whimsical
Enchanted	Radiant	Wise
Expressive	Relaxed	Young
Fed	Respected	_____
Free	Safe	_____
Glowing	Satisfied	_____
Hard	Seen	_____

Journal about the last time that you identified with the words you picked out. Allow yourself time and space to breathe and lie down. Pleasure and desirability are complicated emotions. Note why you identified with the words that you chose.

_____

_____

_____

_____

_____

_____

_____

_____

_____

_____

_____

_____

_____

_____

_____

_____

_____

_____

_____

_____

_____

_____

_____

Which of the words on the list feel accessible to you? Which feel inaccessible?

_____

_____

_____

_____

_____

Did you define attractiveness differently than the other people who were with you in that space?

_____

_____

_____

_____

_____

Were you able to see your beauty before others saw it? Did others see your attractiveness before you were able to? What difference did that make?

_____

_____

_____

_____

_____

How did people react to your beauty? Were you embraced for it? Were you stigmatized?

_____

_____

_____

_____

_____

Beauty Manifesto

Beauty is not a state of being seen but a state of being. Beauty can only arise in situations of deep self-trust and self-compassion. Beauty cannot be improved upon or improved into. Beauty makes us realize that much of what we try to solve with self-improvement is actually healed through self-compassion. Beauty cannot be owned or defined without the joy and agony of sharing both experience and struggle. Beauty must be protected but it cannot be hoarded. Without honesty, beauty disappears. Beauty survives the world and it will outlive the world.

Write your own manifesto about beauty by starting every sentence with the word *Beauty*. Write until you feel satisfied.

Social Anxiety

Social anxiety seems so normal that we forget how much it affects our relationships, our comfort, and our ability to believe in our own dreams.

It's easy to forget that everyone is socially anxious sometimes. There is a tendency, when we are anxious, to think that other people must be fluid, confident, and knowledgeable in unspoken social codes. This is how social anxiety alienates us from those we wish we could know.

There are many types of social anxieties. I've named five types for you here: the anxiety of being with people you don't know, the anxiety of being with people you already know, the anxiety that shows up in the middle of the night, the anxiety of falling in love, and the anxiety of sharing something new about yourself. Anxiety is not an emotion but a condition that afflicts us when we have trouble relaxing into emotion. We tend to feel anxiety when we need distance from our emotions, such as when we are overwhelmed by new people, by love, and by vulnerability.

WHEN YOU ARE AROUND
SOMEONE YOU DON'T KNOW

This is the stereotypical social anxiety—what we usually think of when we think of social anxiety. It's anxiety around strangers, or—more precisely—anxiety around *being* a stranger.

This anxiety is also about cultural belonging. When you meet someone new alongside friends you've had for a long time, you're less anxious about how you are perceived. This is because you know that people know you. When you are entering a completely new environment for the first time, you lack that same level of comfort.

Being the stranger isn't just about the circumstantial situation of meeting new people; it is also about identity. Certain people are seen as more of a stranger than others are. For example, queer people may have more anxiety around being seen as a predator on first dates or around new friend groups and the fear of being excluded. Many of us will have anxiety around job interviews.

When meeting someone for the first time, ask yourself these questions:

You don't know this person at all yet. What ideas or assumptions do you have about them?

_____

_____

_____

_____

_____

_____

_____

_____

_____

What fears are you bringing into your first meetup?

_____

_____

_____

_____

_____

_____

_____

_____

_____

_____

How do those fears feel in your body? If you were to compare yourself to an animal with a good defense system, what animal would you be? (An octopus that swims away? A porcupine that gets spiky? A chameleon that changes color?)

_____

_____

_____

_____

_____

_____

_____

_____

_____

Go through your list of assumptions about that person. Could any of these assumptions be contributing to your fears?

_____

_____

_____

_____

_____

_____

_____

What do you think the defensive animal that you chose needs when it is scared?

_____

_____

_____

_____

_____

_____

How do you think the defensive animal's needs when it is scared translate to your own needs?

_____

_____

_____

_____

_____

_____

WHEN YOU ARE AROUND A GROUP
OF PEOPLE YOU ALREADY KNOW

I call this one "party anxiety." It's the anxiety that comes up when you are around a group of people with whom you have very different relationships. It's the fear that these different people may have different expectations of you. Think about when you bring a personal friend to a workplace party— you might be afraid of seeming too casual with your boss in the room, or of seeming too rigid with your friend watching.

When you hang out with a bunch of people, the stakes are also higher. If you do something embarrassing then, it's very different from doing it with just one person around. If you do it at a party, then it's possible that everyone you know will see it happen. It's normal to feel anxious about gatherings, because you are aware that what you do will affect how people know you.

When hanging out with a group of people, ask yourself these questions:

- Are there people in the group who you are especially anxious about? Or people who you are nervous about meeting each other?

- Will people you know from different places be present at the gathering? How do you feel about that?
- Are you afraid of being embarrassed? What is the most embarrassing thing that could happen? Could this potentially embarrassing thing also become either a teaching moment or a funny moment in hindsight?

WHEN IT'S 3 A.M.

This type of social anxiety doesn't usually come up for me unless I am stoned out of my mind, though it can come up when you are sober. It comes out of nowhere, when you are happily in bed trying to feel warm and cozy and suddenly have the thought, *What if that normal thing I did was actually super wrong?*

When this type of anxiety arises, it is important to remember that there is absolutely nothing to be done. Even if you did something that aggravated another person, it's not your job to worry about their feelings unless they bring it up. If it affects your relationship with them, it is still up to them to describe their own emotions. Most of the time, with this type of social anxiety, it's just your brain freaking out over nothing.

When your brain freaks out in the middle of the night, ask yourself:

- What are you getting out of worrying about this right now?
- If a friend called you in the middle of the night with these same concerns, what would you tell them?
- What is something that you can do to get out of your spiral? (For example, you can masturbate, you can get a midnight snack, or you can get up out of bed and do a quick walk around your block.)

WHEN YOU ARE FALLING IN LOVE

This type of social anxiety is related to limerence. It's not exactly love in practice but the fear that you are falling deeper into your feelings than the other person and that they do not return your feelings. This may show up as anxieties around texting, phone calls, dating, or flirtation.

When you are falling in love with someone, ask yourself:

- How do you feel in your body when you are anxious about this person? What do these feelings make you want to do?
- If you were to verbalize these anxieties, what would they say to you?
- Do you have any wounds around falling in love that are present in your body right now?
- What can you do to celebrate the bigness of your heart, even if that bigness is terrifying right now?

WHEN YOU SHARE
A PART OF YOURSELF THAT YOU
HAVE NOT SHARED BEFORE

You can overwhelm yourself with your own vulnerability. The anxiety that you feel from this may be your body's way of defending you against all of the new emotions that show up when you share something that you have not shared before.

When you are more vulnerable than you are used to in an established relationship, ask yourself:

- Did you mean to share what you shared?
- If so, what were the things about the other person that made you feel safe enough to share? What is causing you to doubt your instincts now?
- If you did not mean to share, do you feel like you broke your own boundaries, or are you afraid that you broke the other person's boundaries? Do you feel that you want to bring up this question of boundaries with them?
- How are you afraid that the new information about you will affect the established relationship?
- How can you address this fear of upsetting an established relationship while still respecting your decision to share what you shared?

Shyness

I wasn't shy until I immigrated. Before I moved to Iowa, I lived in Henan province. I was a young Aries, set to follow the path of my favorite cousin (also an Aries). She was the kind of kid who got in fistfights with neighborhood kids, the kind of kid who aggravated my grandma because her antics led to rocks coming through the windows every now and then. When I was a young Aries in China, I fought kids in playgrounds. I made it clear when I didn't like someone. I yelled at my teachers even when they beat me, as teachers do in China.

Then, I became shy.

When I moved to the United States, I didn't talk for a year. If an adult asked me a question, I would stare until they went away. I learned English quickly, as kids tend to do—that wasn't the problem. The problem was, I was experiencing what it felt like to be a racial minority for the first time in my life.

Venus isn't just about beauty and openness. Venus is about the valuable defenses that you have within relationships. Shyness can be a learned tool. We experience being overwhelmed as children and we find shyness waiting for us. Over time, shyness can change, as we learn more about ourselves and the space we need. This is another way of loving Venus.

Being shy is disorienting. It's scary. It's also precious, and the most tender place to find yourself in. When you're shy as an older person, you remember what it felt like to be a child all at once—not a welcome feeling all the time, but an important one.

When you're shy, you're hypervigilant—you're genuinely not sure whether or not the environment you're in is one where you will be able to build safety. You're not sure if you will find kids who want to play with you. You're not sure if someone who you're falling for will love you back. You're not sure if a job will make you feel shitty.

Shyness can seem like such a quiet emotion, but it's actually a very loud one. It is about having a head full of screaming anxieties—worrying whether someone will like you. Shyness can be about looking for escape plans while feeling like you can't physically move away.

Think about an experience during which you found yourself feeling shy either recently or when you were a kid. Choose an experience that is significant to you. Close your eyes and remember that feeling of shyness.

If you could give words to your shyness,
what do you think it would say to you?

EXAMPLES OF WHAT YOUR SHYNESS IS SAYING

- I'm not sure if this person is ready to receive my vulnerability. I don't know if I can trust my desire.
- All these people seem to already know each other. I don't know if they're willing to accept me.
- I'm afraid that my true self won't be acceptable here. If I get fired again, I don't know what I will do.
- People who are experts in my field don't tend to look like me. I'm afraid that people here will think I'm showing off.

Your shyness exposes your fears and also the moments during which you feel the most tender. Look back at the list of things that you feel your shyness is saying to you, and ask yourself to see the tenderness.

EXAMPLES OF WHAT YOUR SHYNESS IS SAYING

- I really care about this person and I am capable of love.
- I want to survive and I make decisions that give me survival.
- When I talk, people are listening, and that is a new, exciting feeling.
- I am ready for change and just not sure whether it will happen.

Notice when you're doing this reframing exercise above that you're having to go back to specific memories. Ask yourself what you might have wanted to hear at those moments. Notice that, when you feel shy, it is often not helpful to hear someone say "Don't be shy." Your shyness is also a yearning.

THE SPACE TO FEEL SHY

Shyness is often a response to oppression, and you are not your shyness. You are allowed to experience your shyness, and your emotional responses are precious. Protecting your tenderness is often about knowing and empathizing with your defense mechanisms.

We have trouble giving ourselves space to feel shy because we have a lot of trouble giving ourselves space to feel yearning. It can seem cruel to yourself—or irresponsible—to yearn for something that you anticipate not getting.

What does your shyness yearn for? (Circle some words and add your own.)

Acceptance	Freedom	Praise	_____
Affirmation	Love	Protection	_____
Change	Money	_____	_____

What structures make you wish you didn't yearn for the things that you yearn for? Can you spend a little time verbalizing these structures? Examples may include racism, classism, academia, capitalism, your family, your culture, and more.

Artist and writer Hannah Black once wrote on Twitter that she doesn't believe in internalized oppression, that oppression is an external system, and that trying to "fix" your own emotional responses results in a lot of self-blame. This lines up with what I see—I see a lot of people of color talking about our internalized racism, a lot of trans people talking about internalized transphobia, and a lot of working-class people talking about internalized classism, when it should be the opposite: White people should be talking about internalized racism, cis people about internalized transphobia, wealthy people about internalized classism, and so forth.

SHYNESS AND CONTROL

You deserve to have control. You need to have a sense of control, or *agency*, to trust your own choices. You need to have some degree of control over your environment to feel safe. You need control over yourself to feel right in your relationships.

When you desire control that you do not have, what you really desire is change. Change is not always possible on an individual scale, but it is crucial to protect your hope that change is possible, even when you don't see change right away.

Go back to your list of circled and written yearnings and reframe them, translating them into wishes for change.

EXAMPLES OF WISHES FOR CHANGE

- I want this person to see me as a whole being and not through the lens of their assumptions around gender.
- I want to not have to wonder if I am being ostracized because of race.
- I want to change what success means, and what makes it available.
- I am ready for change, and I am assured that change is inevitable.

Accepting Affirmation

The best way to accept a compliment is to simply say "Thank you." This is easier said than done because, in the space between hearing a compliment and getting a chance to respond, your body may be going through a myriad of comfortable and uncomfortable sensations. A lot of the time, it is easier to flinch away from or dismiss a compliment than it is to accept the celebration of you.

Receiving praise is about being pushed into a position of pride. For many people, pride doesn't feel safe and brings up contradictory feelings of shame and humiliation. Prideful postures, like putting your head up in the air or holding your arms out in triumph, can feel disorienting to many of us, especially when we are praised. It's not easy to feel safe in pride.

GETTING ATTENTION

When you are complimented, what emotions come up? Circle any emotions you experienced the last time someone paid you a compliment. Keep in mind that you may experience very contradictory emotions when receiving a compliment.

Anger	Fear	Pride
Closeness	Gratitude	Shame
Courage	Humiliation	Triumph
Detachment	Overwhelm	Yearning

Now, using a different color of ink, do the same for the last time you were called to be accountable. What emotions showed up for you? Did some contradict others?

When you are given a compliment, acknowledge the work that the praise is calling your attention to.

COMPLIMENTS

What is the compliment calling your attention to?

ACCOUNTABILITY-ASKS

What is the accountability-ask calling your attention to?

CENTER ATTACHMENT,
NOT WORTHINESS

Remember—a compliment will never describe your inherent worthiness. That is because your worthiness—whether you deserve to live, thrive, and find relief—is unquestionable. Instead, a compliment describes your attachment with a person or group and can help you envision what a positive attachment might look like.

If you have trouble feeling safe in positive attachments, you might feel very uncomfortable receiving compliments. That's okay.

Here are some questions to use, to journal, pull tarot cards, or start a conversation with someone who has praised you.

What is the compliment calling your attention to?

What did it take for your relationship to get to a place where that person is able to give you praise?

What does a positive relationship with the compliment giver create the potential for?

TROUBLED COMPLIMENTS

Sometimes, a compliment feels "off" to us because we disagree with another person's perception of us; it's not who we think we are. We might worry that someone is misgendering us, idealizing us, or fetishizing us in their compliment. We worry that they are not trying to form a relationship with us, but instead with their idea of who we are.

When this happens, remind yourself that you are *not* helpless in the face of another person's perception of you. In the same way that a compliment is about the quality of attachment and not about who you intrinsically are, a compliment describes the compliment giver's perception of the world more than it describes your essential identity.

Create an "I am" poem by completing twenty sentences that begin with "I am":

I AM _____

_____

I AM _____

_____

I AM _____

_____

I AM _____

_____

I AM _____

_____

I AM _____

_____

I AM _____

_____

I AM _____

_____

I AM _____

_____

I AM _____

_____

I AM _____

_____

I AM _____

_____

I AM _____

_____

I AM _____

_____

I AM _____

_____

I AM _____

_____

I AM _____

_____

I AM _____

_____

I AM _____

_____

I AM _____

_____

What emotions showed up during your completion of the "I am" poem? How do those emotions feel physically?

_____

_____

_____

_____

_____

_____

_____

_____

_____

_____

_____

_____

_____

When a person misperceives you, when that misperception becomes evident through a well-meaning compliment, this shows that there is something in the relationship that you have with this person that you'd like to change. It is up to you whether you want to do the work of this change. You are never obligated to attach more strongly to someone just because they complimented you.

If you do want to strengthen your attachment to someone who misperceived you, you will have to interrupt their perception of you. Sometimes it takes only a gentle nudge or joke to change it. Other times, a much longer conversation is needed.

Complete the following sentences as many times as you'd like—however many times it takes to satisfy you.

ACCEPTING COMPLIMENTS gives me more potential to praise others.

ACCEPTING COMPLIMENTS allows me to understand the depth of my effort.

ACCEPTING COMPLIMENTS helps me find safety in pride.

ACCEPTING COMPLIMENTS _____

_____

_____

ACCEPTING COMPLIMENTS _____

_____

_____

ACCEPTING COMPLIMENTS _____

_____

_____

ACCEPTING COMPLIMENTS _____

_____

_____

ACCEPTING COMPLIMENTS _____

_____

_____

ACCEPTING COMPLIMENTS _____

_____

_____

ACCEPTING COMPLIMENTS _____

_____

_____

MARS
RETURN

FREQUENCY	SIGNIFICANCE	WHEN IT HAPPENS
Occurs approximately every two years	Anxiety, conflict, thwarted mobility, anger, simplification	Begins when Mars is farther than approximately 120 degrees from the Sun

MARS RETURNS BREAK YOU OPEN. Mars returns happen when transiting Mars returns to the same place it held at your birth. They tend to happen every two years or so and they hit some people harder than others. Mars returns can feel like emergencies; they can coincide with moves or conflict. When your Mars returns, go back to who you were two years prior and do some remembering.

Mars returns are part of the cycle that transiting Mars makes to your natal placement. A few months after a Mars return, Mars will make a square or a 90 degree aspect to your natal Mars. A few months after that, transiting Mars will oppose your natal chart. Then it squares itself again before returning once more.

You can find the dates of your Mars returns, squares, and opposition periods by consulting an ephemeris (this is a book that tells you where all of the given ingresses of a given period will be).

Reflecting on Your
Last Mars Cycle

What were the dates of your last Mars return? Who were you two years ago during your last Mars return?

_____

_____

_____

_____

_____

Have you been forced to let go of anything from that time that appeared vital to you then?

_____

_____

_____

_____

_____

How do you grieve the loss of the thing that once appeared vital to you?

_____

_____

_____

_____

_____

What were the dates of the first Mars square directly after the return? Who were you during that time period?

_____

_____

_____

_____

_____

_____

_____

What were the dates of your last Mars opposition? Who were you during that time period?

_____

_____

_____

_____

_____

_____

_____

What were the dates of the Mars square directly after the opposition? Who were you during that time period?

_____

_____

_____

_____

_____

_____

Anger

Anger is often associated with Mars, the god of war. When I talk with people about anger, I ask them, "How were you taught anger?" "What does anger feel like in your body?" "What do you do when you're mad about something?" And, always: "What are you angry about?"

I find that we spend a lot of time talking about the emotions *around* anger rather than the anger itself. Anger is an emotion that is easy to identify with and one that might need its own protection. Emotions related to anger—perhaps surprisingly so—are feelings of disconnection, attachment, fear, and guilt. While feeling anger at someone or something, you may, at the same time, be feeling afraid of your anger, just as you were afraid of a parent when you were a child. You might also feel guilt with the anger.

Anger knows exactly what it is trying to do. But it can be hard to believe in our emotions. For example, when talking about our anger, we discuss why we are mad but we also talk about why we feel that we should *not* be mad. We talk about what we see, what we feel, and what those things make us want to do—but we also talk about the doubt of living life as ourselves and only ourselves. We wonder if our emotions are getting in the way of our compassion. We wonder if the other person sees it differently. We wonder if we are triggered, and we wonder whether this feeling of anger is something to adjust in ourselves, in privacy, without making our narratives public.

It is hard to believe in our own emotions. Empathy makes emotions real. Empathy has the power to make doubtful stories seem truer. A lot of the time, our anger does not need to be "right." Our anger needs empathy.

LITERALIZING ANGER

Anger is a physical reaction and an automatic one, just like eating or shitting or breathing. To notice our anger, it is important to notice the ways it affects our bodies.

Find your symptoms of anger here. For some people, anger affects the heart and results in chest pain. For others, it is around the stomach and skin, resulting in stomach pain and chills. Some feel it in their muscles, like they have to stand up and run away when they are angry. When you are angry, how does it affect your . . .

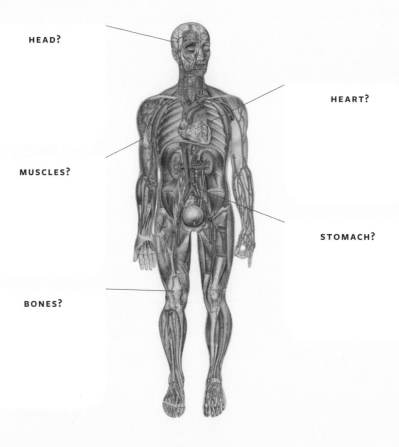

HEAD?

HEART?

MUSCLES?

STOMACH?

BONES?

Draw shapes and colors to represent your responses to the following:

Does anger burn or does it feel cold?

Does anger make it harder to sit still or does it make you unable to move?

Do you get loud or become quiet?

Do you become angry right away or does your anger have a delayed reaction?

Do you tend to ignore your anger or let it overcome you?

Reflect on five ways that your family showed anger when you were growing up. How did you know when your mom was mad at you, for example? What did you do when you were upset with your sibling?

ONE

TWO

THREE

FOUR

FIVE

Let yourself know whether you think this behavior still works for you or not, and why. Complete the sections below.

How you showed your anger today		Was this display of anger learned as an adult or as a kid?
	$\longrightarrow$	
	$\longrightarrow$	
	$\longrightarrow$	
	$\longrightarrow$	

Anger and fear are twins. Sometimes one is easier to recognize than the other.

Something that made you angry	What your anger is protecting you from	Any fear attached to your anger
$\longrightarrow$	$\longrightarrow$	
_____	_____	_____
$\longrightarrow$	$\longrightarrow$	
_____	_____	_____
$\longrightarrow$	$\longrightarrow$	
_____	_____	_____
$\longrightarrow$	$\longrightarrow$	
_____	_____	_____

If you feel ready to process anger from your childhood, complete the following exercise. You do not have to be willing to process someone else's anger for them, especially when it's a parent or an authority figure's anger. However, if you *want* to translate anger that was directed at you as a child into fear for yourself, you can use this exercise. Usually, when we translate anger into fear, we are exercising an extraordinary amount of empathy. You are in control of whether you want to hold empathy and for whom. Understanding what the angry people we experienced as children were afraid of can often help you empathize with your most critical parts.

Instances when an adult was angry
at you as a child

What that adult or you might
have been afraid of

$\longrightarrow$

_____   _____

$\longrightarrow$

_____   _____

$\longrightarrow$

_____   _____

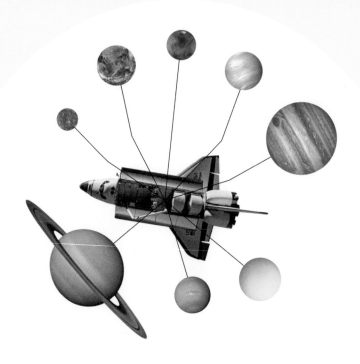

BUILDING AN
ANGER TOOLKIT

In a box, folder, or drawer, build a toolkit of items that will be easily accessible to you when you are angry. Don't let these items spill over into your regular space but keep them sealed off from the rest of your room. This isn't because your anger should be hidden but because it is a vulnerable emotion that needs protection. When you process anger, you want to make sure that it feels special and sacred.

Some items in your anger toolkit might include:

A SMALL NOTEBOOK

This is your anger journal. Decorate it however you want. When you are angry, you will write down in this journal what happened and why you are angry.

A PILLOW

This is your anger pillow. Feel free to punch or scream into the pillow when you are angry.

JOKES

Making jokes about the things that make you most angry can be a way to validate your emotions while inducing a cathartic emotional release.

SOME PAPER AND A MARKER

You can write things that make you angry down on this paper and burn it somewhere safely (see the New Moon Removal Ritual, page 20).

In this toolkit of easily accessible items, keep a sheet of paper that feels different than all the other items. On this piece of paper, make your anger wish list. Write down on this sheet of paper all of the things that you wish you could do or have when you are angry. These should be things that are not easily accessible to you. Keep this sheet of paper to remind yourself that it is okay to want things that aren't immediately accessible.

Building
Physical Safety

There are a lot of reasons why we might feel physically unsafe when we are not facing an active danger. Maybe the social situation we are in reminds us of a past one in which we were hurt. We might remember danger when we have sex with someone, even when we want to have sex with them.

This section of the book is for people who are in situations where they need to remind themselves of their safety but are experiencing trouble finding physical safety. It is not for those who are in situations facing active danger.

TAKE A BREAK

When your body feels that it is in danger, even if you know cognitively that you are not, you may have a reaction of wanting to get away from the source of the danger. You can remind yourself of your consent by showing it to yourself physically: Stop the sex. Take a break. Remind yourself that you have the option of continuing after the break or not. Even if you know that you want to continue having sex, give yourself a short five-minute break—during which you and your partner shift to a more platonic pose or do something that you usually do together, like watching a funny video—before choosing to continue. This can help your body realize that you are not doing something because you have to do it, but because you choose to.

If you're ever in a room where you start feeling physically unsafe, taking a break might mean letting yourself leave for just a few minutes. It can also mean choosing not to be in the room. When you feel physically unsafe, you always have the option of reacting with the emotion and leaving a room that's causing you distress. Leaving temporarily and coming back can also be a way to show yourself your consent. You are also always allowed to leave without coming back.

What emotions does the possibility of leaving bring up for you?

_____

_____

_____

_____

_____

Is there anything that holds you back from leaving?

_____

_____

_____

_____

_____

Are the things that hold you back from leaving important? How might you acknowledge their importance?

_____

_____

_____

_____

_____

BREATHING

You can do this method in stealth, when you are intimate with someone, or you can ask for a break to refocus your attention on your body. Sometimes, if you're kissing or making out with someone, it can be easy to feel short of breath.

Focus on your heartbeat and breath. Notice how long it takes you, with this focus, to get to a place of easy, deep breathing. If that is enough for you to find stability, you can keep going and continue sex.

If you want, you can also take a break from sex to do more complicated breathing sounds. If you're in a room where you're feeling unsafe, you can either do these sounds right there in the room under your breath or move to a place where no one hears you. Making sounds while breathing is a way to regulate your nervous system. Because fear is a physical emotion, sound making can be a powerful way to change your experience of fear.

These are six healing sounds (Liù Zì Jué) that are around 1,500 years old:

嘘 **xū** (sounds like a sigh you make by pointing your tongue and pushing it toward the front of your mouth): This sound supports your liver, where anger is stored. Making this sound on an exhale will help you regulate anger.

呵 **hē** (almost like a guttural hiss, done by curling your tongue and pushing the middle section of it toward the roof of your mouth): This sound supports your heart, where love and cruelty live. Making this sound on an exhale will help you regulate love and cruelty.

呼 **hū** (make your mouth into a tunnel): This sound supports your spleen, where you store anxiety. Making this sound on an exhale will help you regulate anxiety.

嘶 **sī** (flatten your lips and push your teeth together): This sound supports your lungs, where sorrow and grief are stored. Making this sound on an exhale will help you regulate sorrow and grief.

吹 **chuī** (made by pushing the tip of the tongue up and pushing air through the lips—this sound is made through several consecutive puffs and not all at once): This sound supports your kidneys, where fear lives. Making this sound on a staccato beat on an exhale will help you regulate fear.

嘻 **xī** (a little like 嘶 sī, except the tongue is farther back with the middle against the roof of the mouth): This sound supports your life. Make this sound on an exhale when you want to remind yourself of the miraculousness of your life.

Is it possible to feel anger inside your body or does it feel like an external presence?

_____

_____

_____

_____

_____

_____

_____

Where in your body do you feel anger the most?

_____

_____

_____

_____

_____

How do these places change when you breathe deeply?

_____

_____

_____

_____

_____

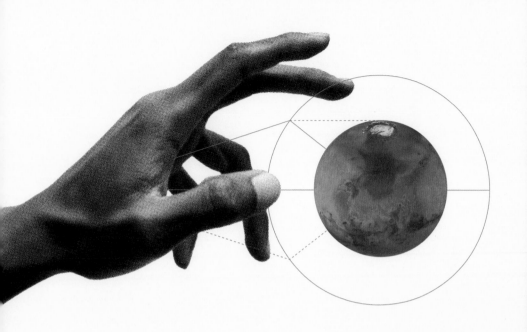

PHYSICAL TOUCH

Most of our emotions are not in our heads but in our bodies. More specifically, there is a long nerve called the vagus nerve that runs through your chest and attaches to your belly, whose purpose is emotional regulation. That is why some feelings, like shock or disgust or fear, have such a direct effect on our hearts and stomachs.

Put your hand against your sternum, skin to skin, and rub yourself a little. Put your hand against your belly and massage it in circles.

When you're in a room where you're feeling unsafe, you can slip your hand into the neck of your shirt or release one button from a collared shirt. You can do this while talking with someone or sitting by yourself.

What does it feel like to give yourself physical support?

_____

_____

_____

_____

_____

_____

Is it easier to accept support from yourself or externally from other people or others' ideas?

_____

_____

_____

_____

_____

Where in your body do you feel this support the most?

_____

_____

_____

_____

_____

_____

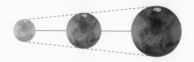

MAKE YOURSELF PHYSICALLY LARGER

Adjust your arms and legs so that you are in a victory or conquering pose. During sex, this might look like shifting to a more active position where you can move more freely. It might look like getting on top. It might look like playfully pinning your partner down or even standing up with your feet apart and moving back into touch from an upright position.

Sometimes, we feel aggression when we are scared. Healthy aggression is the antidote to shame. It is normal for survivors to find themselves feeling angry or aggressive during sex. If your partner is into it, exploring kink and letting yourself perform aggression during sex can be a great way to regulate feelings of shame.

If you are feeling unsafe in a room, standing with a more upright posture, with a wider stance, and with arms positioned around your waist area can help regulate you. If you are in a room where there is a higher area, moving to that area can make you feel physically larger. Holding your chin up high and posturing your heart out, opening it up, can make you feel bigger.

When does it feel okay to be aggressive?

_____

_____

_____

_____

_____

_____

Are there any moments when it does not feel okay?

_____

_____

_____

_____

_____

_____

_____

_____

_____

_____

What do your answers to the first two questions tell you about your survival?

_____

_____

_____

_____

_____

_____

_____

_____

_____

_____

_____

VOCALIZING

Vocalizing, making sounds with your body that assert your aliveness and survival, can help physically regulate you when your body thinks that it is in danger even when you know that you are not. Your voice is powerful. When you vocalize your anger, you're letting other people—and yourself—know that you are here and powerful.

When you're feeling fear in a room, you might feel a little self-conscious talking out loud. You do not need to speak out loud to other people in order for your voice to feel powerful. Going into a bathroom and speaking to your-self, talking with a friend who is outside of the situation, or journaling can often be enough for your voice to feel adequately expressive.

Are there any specific words that are important to you when expressing anger? What are they?

When is it easy to vocalize anger? What do challenges feel like in your throat?

_____

_____

_____

_____

_____

_____

Is it ever important for someone specific to hear you?

_____

_____

_____

_____

_____

_____

Is it ever not necessary for anyone to hear you?

_____

_____

_____

_____

_____

_____

Standing Up for Yourself

The first thing to do when you stand up for yourself is a playful physical exercise that releases anxiety. Anxiety works to cover up the emotions you are feeling and can lead to chronic pain or illnesses.

Conflict is creative. When conflict happens, invite yourself into a creative state of being so that you are able to see all of the options available.

Try this exercise, which is adapted from somatic therapist and educator Peter Levine's Somatic Experiencing exercise on anxiety and qigong techniques.

- In order to release anxiety, hold your shoulders up high so that your neck is hidden. Clench up your body. You might bring your knees up if you are sitting or look down with your gaze. Pretend that you are a turtle who is trying to hide. This is a fear pose. Hold your pose.
- Suddenly, let your shoulders fall down and your body relax.

What emotions were exposed when you dropped your shoulders and relaxed your body? Circle any that apply or add your own:

Anger	Excitement	Frustration	Profoundness
Arousal	Exhaustion	Irritation	Relief
Disgust	Exhilaration	Joy	_____
Dread	Fear	Laughter	_____

Now, stand up and place your feet apart in a wide stance. Your feet should be wider than your shoulders. Bring your hands up, palms facing down, until they are high above your head. Slowly, bring your hands down while holding your elbows out and squatting down slightly until you are almost in a chair pose. Pretend that you are a bear who is trying to protect themselves. This is a fighting pose. Hold this pose.

Slowly, bring your hands up high again, back the way they came, and then back down. Place both palms against your tummy protectively.

What emotions did you feel in the fighting pose? Circle any that apply or add your own:

Anger	Exhaustion	Joy
Arousal	Exhilaration	Laughter
Disgust	Fear	Relief
Dread	Frustration	_____
Excitement	Interest	_____
	Irritation	

Which position felt more familiar, the fear pose or the fighting pose?

_____

_____

_____

_____

_____

_____

_____

_____

Did either of the positions feel safe or unsafe?

_____

_____

_____

_____

_____

_____

_____

Was it easier for you to maintain the fear posture or the fighting posture?

_____

_____

_____

_____

_____

_____

If you have a pet, did the pet react to seeing you in either of the postures?

_____

_____

_____

_____

_____

_____

_____

DOGS AS MARS REMEDIATION

Remediation is the practice of caring for your chart. It often happens with ritual, art, story, or relationship—all of the things that life is made up of. Dogs and relationships to dogs are a form of Mars remediation. If you have an afflicted Mars (Mars in Taurus, Cancer, or Libra; Mars in hard aspect with Saturn; Mars in hard aspect with Jupiter; isolated Mars in your chart), being around dogs, making friends with dogs around you, serving at a dog shelter, or raising dogs yourself can be a great way to externalize and support your Mars.

Dogs will pick up on your tension and anxiety even when you're not aware of it yourself. They might bark when they sense that you are anxious. Your aggression is a little like a dog that is trying to protect you. And you can learn to care for your aggression by caring for a dog.

WHEN YOUR AGGRESSION KEEPS BARKING

- **Keep your aggression entertained** with playfully aggressive games. Games that are playfully aggressive include: pillow fights, tag, boxing, splashing in a pool, "rage rooms" where you smash everything, shoelace or sock fights (where you try to untie someone's shoelace or take their socks off).

- **Touch**—Rarely, dogs stop barking when you bark back. A dog who has gone to dog school might learn to stop when you ask it to, but most of the dogs I have met stop barking when you put a comforting hand on their head. You can practice putting your own hand on your head gently to self-soothe.

- **Show consistency**—Your aggression needs consistent play and consistent care just like dogs need consistent play and consistent care.

The next thing that you're going to do to stand up for yourself is to decide what impact you'd like to have. Decide what defines a victory for you.

For example, if you find that you are constantly being denied time off from work, a victory might take the form of a policy change instead of one approved day off. A victory might also be larger or smaller than you anticipated. If you are constantly navigating conflict with a family member, a victory might look like hearing yourself say "You can't treat me like this" out loud. Your victory might not look like typical ideas of what it looks like to be victorious, such as conquering or winning. If you are standing up to sexual violence, building a network of survivors might be a victory. A victory is anything that reminds you that you are able to make an impact on the world.

Remember that when you achieve your victory, your conflict is done even when a struggle that you are engaged in is still ongoing. It is important to take time to celebrate victories because celebration of victories are powerful. Celebrations disrupt just as much as fighting does. Celebrating also helps you pause your healthy aggression so that you are not overwhelmed by one conflict. It might feel tempting to chase revenge when you feel victorious, but not only will it invite revenge against you, it will distract you from your larger struggle and the pleasure of living life.

When you practice standing up for yourself, make sure that you act at a time when you feel like your desired impact is possible. That might look like choosing to talk with a friend on a weekend and not a weekday when you know both of you are too exhausted from work to listen if your desired impact is to be heard by them. It might look like making sure that there is a witness to you standing up to a family member if victory to you means that you no longer have to mediate family conflicts alone.

WRITE DOWN YOUR DESIRED IMPACT HERE

My victory looks like . . .

How much time and energy do you want to put into a conflict? Include the time spent on thinking about and acting on the conflict.

What might tell you when you are too tired for conflict?

How can you keep yourself accountable to your own boundaries in a conflict?

How might your aggression feel when it is denied the conflict that it wants? What might it need then?

SOLIDARITY

Have you done work that is similar to the work that you are getting ready to do within your conflict? Do you have experience with similar conflicts?

Is there work that has already been done within the struggle that you are engaged in? Where is that work being done, and who is doing the work?

What will make you feel less alone in your struggle?

CREATIVE CONFLICT

What makes you feel most creative these days?

What might bringing that creativity to your conflict look like?

What might being playful in conflict look like?

Are there any options to move forward that you didn't see before
that you do when you bring your creative self into the conflict?

JUPITER RETURN

FREQUENCY	SIGNIFICANCE	WHEN IT HAPPENS
Occurs approximately every 12 years	Confusion, imagination, breakages, freedom, synchronicity	Begins when Jupiter returns to the sign of your natal Jupiter and ends when Jupiter leaves that sign

JUPITER RETURNS HAPPEN ONCE EVERY TWELVE YEARS. The first one you get, you're at the onset of puberty. There's a lot of pressure around Jupiter returns, with astrologers describing the time as being about expansion, wealth, and travel, but the best way to describe it is as a time of bewilderment.

Jupiter returns when we go through our worst breakups, quit our jobs, and are left wondering who we are. Jupiter return is when you question all of the things you believe, and you're left wondering whether you truly believe in anything at all.

Jupiter returns tend to correspond to first house profection years (the ages at which your annual ruler also rules the first house. This happens every twelve years), which happen to be the times in your life when you break your identity down and restart from scratch. People tend to give birth or abort things during Jupiter returns. The fifth Jupiter return overlaps with a Saturn return.

The first thing to do with a Jupiter return is to sit down and remember your last Jupiter cycle. The return closes one Jupiter cycle before it starts another.

Reflecting on Your Last Jupiter Cycle

What were the dates of your last Jupiter return?
Ages when your Jupiter returns, loosely, are: 12, 24, 36, 48, 60, 72, 84, 96, and 108.

How did being that age change your life? What was life like at that age?

What was your last Jupiter opposition like? You would count 6 years after your last Jupiter return. Jupiter oppositions tend to happen, loosely, around the ages of:
6, 18, 30, 42, 54, 66, 78, 90, 102.

Are there any things that you started during your last Jupiter return that reached a culmination point during your last Jupiter opposition?

_____

_____

_____

_____

_____

_____

_____

How do you feel about those things now?

_____

_____

_____

_____

_____

_____

Do you want to bring those things into your next Jupiter cycle? How do you want those things to change?

_____

_____

_____

_____

_____

_____

JUPITER RETURN
EXERCISES

MAKE A JOKE OUT OF YOUR HUBRIS

Think of the things you believe yourself to truly be an expert in and find
a way to make fun of your so-called expertise.

In your head, narrate the decisions that you make in your morning commute
in the third person and find what is funny about them.

Create a mini stand-up routine that laughs at the things you
take too seriously in your life.

TAKE OUT A WHITEBOARD AND MAKE A LIST OF ALL THE THINGS YOU DON'T KNOW

Go for at least a hundred.

───────────────

Give yourself extra points for things that you can never find the answer for, like, "Where is the edge of the universe?" or "What do dogs dream about?"

───────────────

Put the board up somewhere in your home and look at it every day.

PLAN A TRIP

If you are able to go around the world, then go around the world.

───────────────

If you can't go that far, take a day trip or go to a neighborhood you've never been to before.

───────────────

Go as far outside of your comfort zone as time and money allow you to go right now.

───────────────

Make a list of places you want to go that aren't accessible to you at the moment.

FIND A FIELD, AND RUN AS FAR AS YOU CAN INTO THE HORIZON UNTIL YOU ARE OUT OF BREATH.

Notice how little you have moved.

───────────────

Remember how big the world is.

Supporting Your Imagination, Foolishness, and Dreams

TAKE A BREAK FROM REASON

Reason is about sensible decision-making. It's about figuring out how to move all of your things—what boxes you can use, how you're going to make the effort—because you've decided to move in with a lover. It's about figuring out who will take care of your cat because you want to go on a trip. Reason is *not* about that leap of faith, of deciding to move in with a lover or to go somewhere you've never been.

There's a time and a place for reason. It's unsuitable for dreaming. Allowing yourself to be dictated to by reason is allowing yourself to only do things when they are most practical. Some things will never be practical to do. And sometimes you don't need them to be.

IN ORDER TO COUNTER YOUR REASON,
MAKE A LIST OF TEN UNREASONABLE DREAMS

ONE

SIX

TWO

SEVEN

THREE

EIGHT

FOUR

NINE

FIVE

TEN

Philip K. Dick defines reality as that which doesn't go away when we stop believing in it. Angela Davis reminds us that we must always be willing to believe that the impossible is possible. Beliefs are not about reality. They're about creating a reality that is different from all possible versions of reality. They're about magic.

MAKE A LIST OF TEN UNANSWERABLE QUESTIONS

Here are some examples:

What was the first living thing? How big is the universe and what is its shape? What will happen tomorrow?

ONE	SIX
TWO	SEVEN
THREE	EIGHT
FOUR	NINE
FIVE	TEN

Where could you go or what could you do that would expose you to more unanswerable questions?

_____

_____

_____

_____

_____

_____

Where could you go or what could you do that would allow you to exist without knowing who you could become?

_____

_____

_____

_____

_____

_____

What parts of you need healing from the person who you thought you needed to be?

_____

_____

_____

_____

_____

_____

PROTECTING FOOLISHNESS

Oppressed peoples are forced to understand the boundaries around their oppression and to examine the methods through which they are oppressed. We are forced to learn our own oppressions, to plan for them, and to try to predict them. This knowledge is a survival skill. It can also become an endless game of prediction, planning, and strategizing.

Being foolish, like many of those things that we call privileges, is actually a basic need. Like food, water, or shelter, being allowed to be foolish or to appear foolish safely is an essential part of living. A student of mine, Chayu, taught me this. She talked about how only straight men are allowed foolishness when falling in love. The rest of us must be guarded against and prepared for love.

What are some things that make you feel like a happy fool?

What do you allow when you allow foolishness?

_____

_____

_____

_____

_____

_____

_____

_____

_____

_____

How might you protect and nurture your foolishness?

_____

_____

_____

_____

_____

_____

_____

_____

_____

_____

_____

_____

NURTURING DREAMS

Imagine a scenario with me: You're a kindergarten teacher, working with kids who are just starting out their lives. One of your students, a five-year-old, tells you that they are going to become an astronaut and walk through the stars. Upon hearing this, do you:

1 Question the realism of the kid's dream?
2 Ask the kid whether or not they have the qualifications that becoming an astronaut would require?
3 Tell the kid, "That's a nice thought," and say nothing more?
4 Give the kid age-appropriate books, videos, and other resources about space?

If, as a kindergarten teacher, you chose options one or two, what do you think would happen? If the kid in question has other supportive adults in their life, such as a parent or an older sibling, those adults might give you a talking-to in defense of that child! Why? Because, by dismissing the child's dream and focusing only on their lack of qualification, you are not doing your job as a teacher, which is to acknowledge, understand, and support that child's *potential*.

Let me ask you some questions: When you find yourself in the rare condition of having a dream, what do you do for yourself? Do you fixate on your lack of qualification? Do you question how realistic the dream is? Do you enjoy the dream as a nice thought that probably won't amount to much unless something calls you out of passivity? Or, do you actively support your potential by enjoying what the dream exposes you to?

Cynicism makes us focus on results. It makes us focus on outcomes. But dream connoisseurs know that dreams are best enjoyed through tangent.

Go back to your list of "unreasonable" dreams on page 131, which may include anything from conversing with cats to finishing that short story you started five years ago, and make a list of three things that each dream might expose you to. There is space for more unreasonable dreams you might think of later as well. In Yoshihiro Togashi's *Hunter x Hunter*, Ging tells Gon that adventure is not about getting from point A to point B but about "the friends you make along the way." This is why you must always pursue goals that you aren't qualified for and don't have the money to go after. Your dreams may expose you to things that you never set out to pursue, such as: making a new friend, remembering to dance, or walking a new trail. Remember—we aren't focusing on outcomes, qualifications, or even actions right now. All we are paying attention to is the curiosity that the act of dreaming nurtures for us.

"UNREASONABLE" DREAM #1:

Strange and unexpected thing this unreasonable dream might expose you to:

1. _____

2. _____

3. _____

"UNREASONABLE" DREAM #2:

Strange and unexpected thing this unreasonable dream might expose you to:

1. _____

2. _____

3. _____

"UNREASONABLE" DREAM #3:

Strange and unexpected thing this unreasonable dream might expose you to:

1. _____

2. _____

3. _____

"UNREASONABLE" DREAM #4:

Strange and unexpected thing this unreasonable dream might expose you to:

1. _____

2. _____

3. _____

"UNREASONABLE" DREAM #5:

Strange and unexpected thing this unreasonable dream might expose you to:

1. _____

2. _____

3. _____

"UNREASONABLE" DREAM #6:

Strange and unexpected thing this unreasonable dream might expose you to:

1. _____

2. _____

3. _____

"UNREASONABLE" DREAM #7:

Strange and unexpected thing this unreasonable dream might expose you to:

1. _____

2. _____

3. _____

"UNREASONABLE" DREAM #8:

Strange and unexpected thing this unreasonable dream might expose you to:

1. _____

2. _____

3. _____

"UNREASONABLE" DREAM #9:

Strange and unexpected thing this unreasonable dream might expose you to:

1. _____

2. _____

3. _____

"UNREASONABLE" DREAM #10:

Strange and unexpected thing this unreasonable dream might expose you to:

1. _____

2. _____

3. _____

"UNREASONABLE" DREAM #11:
Strange and unexpected thing this unreasonable dream might expose you to:

1. _____

2. _____

3. _____

"UNREASONABLE" DREAM #12:
Strange and unexpected thing this unreasonable dream might expose you to:

1. _____

2. _____

3. _____

"UNREASONABLE" DREAM #13:
Strange and unexpected thing this unreasonable dream might expose you to:

1. _____

2. _____

3. _____

"UNREASONABLE" DREAM #14:
Strange and unexpected thing this unreasonable dream might expose you to:

1. _____

2. _____

3. _____

"UNREASONABLE" DREAM #15:
Strange and unexpected thing this unreasonable dream might expose you to:

1. _____

2. _____

3. _____

"UNREASONABLE" DREAM #16:

Strange and unexpected thing this unreasonable dream might expose you to:

1. _____
2. _____
3. _____

"UNREASONABLE" DREAM #17:

Strange and unexpected thing this unreasonable dream might expose you to:

1. _____
2. _____
3. _____

"UNREASONABLE" DREAM #18:

Strange and unexpected thing this unreasonable dream might expose you to:

1. _____
2. _____
3. _____

"UNREASONABLE" DREAM #19:

Strange and unexpected thing this unreasonable dream might expose you to:

1. _____
2. _____
3. _____

"UNREASONABLE" DREAM #20:

Strange and unexpected thing this unreasonable dream might expose you to:

1. _____
2. _____
3. _____

"UNREASONABLE" DREAM #21:

Strange and unexpected thing this unreasonable dream might expose you to:

1. _____

2. _____

3. _____

"UNREASONABLE" DREAM #22:

Strange and unexpected thing this unreasonable dream might expose you to:

1. _____

2. _____

3. _____

"UNREASONABLE" DREAM #23:

Strange and unexpected thing this unreasonable dream might expose you to:

1. _____

2. _____

3. _____

"UNREASONABLE" DREAM #24:

Strange and unexpected thing this unreasonable dream might expose you to:

1. _____

2. _____

3. _____

"UNREASONABLE" DREAM #25:

Strange and unexpected thing this unreasonable dream might expose you to:

1. _____

2. _____

3. _____

"UNREASONABLE" DREAM #26:

Strange and unexpected thing this unreasonable dream might expose you to:

1. _____

2. _____

3. _____

"UNREASONABLE" DREAM #27:

Strange and unexpected thing this unreasonable dream might expose you to:

1. _____

2. _____

3. _____

"UNREASONABLE" DREAM #28:

Strange and unexpected thing this unreasonable dream might expose you to:

1. _____

2. _____

3. _____

"UNREASONABLE" DREAM #29:

Strange and unexpected thing this unreasonable dream might expose you to:

1. _____

2. _____

3. _____

"UNREASONABLE" DREAM #30:

Strange and unexpected thing this unreasonable dream might expose you to:

1. _____

2. _____

3. _____

"UNREASONABLE" DREAM #31:

Strange and unexpected thing this unreasonable dream might expose you to:

1. _____

2. _____

3. _____

"UNREASONABLE" DREAM #32:

Strange and unexpected thing this unreasonable dream might expose you to:

1. _____

2. _____

3. _____

"UNREASONABLE" DREAM #33:

Strange and unexpected thing this unreasonable dream might expose you to:

1. _____

2. _____

3. _____

"UNREASONABLE" DREAM #34:

Strange and unexpected thing this unreasonable dream might expose you to:

1. _____

2. _____

3. _____

"UNREASONABLE" DREAM #35:

Strange and unexpected thing this unreasonable dream might expose you to:

1. _____

2. _____

3. _____

"UNREASONABLE" DREAM #36:
Strange and unexpected thing this unreasonable dream might expose you to:

1. _____
2. _____
3. _____

"UNREASONABLE" DREAM #37:
Strange and unexpected thing this unreasonable dream might expose you to:

1. _____
2. _____
3. _____

"UNREASONABLE" DREAM #38:
Strange and unexpected thing this unreasonable dream might expose you to:

1. _____
2. _____
3. _____

"UNREASONABLE" DREAM #39:
Strange and unexpected thing this unreasonable dream might expose you to:

1. _____
2. _____
3. _____

"UNREASONABLE" DREAM #40:
Strange and unexpected thing this unreasonable dream might expose you to:

1. _____
2. _____
3. _____

"UNREASONABLE" DREAM #41:
Strange and unexpected thing this unreasonable dream might expose you to:

1. _____

2. _____

3. _____

"UNREASONABLE" DREAM #42:
Strange and unexpected thing this unreasonable dream might expose you to:

1. _____

2. _____

3. _____

"UNREASONABLE" DREAM #43:
Strange and unexpected thing this unreasonable dream might expose you to:

1. _____

2. _____

3. _____

"UNREASONABLE" DREAM #44:
Strange and unexpected thing this unreasonable dream might expose you to:

1. _____

2. _____

3. _____

"UNREASONABLE" DREAM #45:
Strange and unexpected thing this unreasonable dream might expose you to:

1. _____

2. _____

3. _____

"UNREASONABLE" DREAM #46:

Strange and unexpected thing this unreasonable dream might expose you to:

1. _____

2. _____

3. _____

"UNREASONABLE" DREAM #47:

Strange and unexpected thing this unreasonable dream might expose you to:

1. _____

2. _____

3. _____

"UNREASONABLE" DREAM #48:

Strange and unexpected thing this unreasonable dream might expose you to:

1. _____

2. _____

3. _____

"UNREASONABLE" DREAM #49:

Strange and unexpected thing this unreasonable dream might expose you to:

1. _____

2. _____

3. _____

"UNREASONABLE" DREAM #50:

Strange and unexpected thing this unreasonable dream might expose you to:

1. _____

2. _____

3. _____

Following Genius

Jupiter is a planet that doesn't really force you to do things that you don't want to do. It will most likely leave you to your own devices. In fact, Jupiter hates goals and hates effort. The things you find when working with Jupiter don't usually show up as a result of effort. Instead, they are acts of indulgence, of play, and of wandering.

Wu wei is a philosophy that is anti-discipline and anti-effort. Sometimes, it's translated as being about nonviolence or non-action. That's not necessarily what *wu wei* means. *Wei* is one word for Confucian power. Another word for power is *wen*. While wei typically refers to martial power or military strength, wen is more bureaucratic and stately. A Confucian reading of wu wei is not about using military power to rule; instead, it's about using bureaucracy and soft power. In Taoism, wu wei is about not trying to force control over what is not in your control. Wu wei is about observation, paying attention, and strengthening yourself.

Wu wei isn't about not thinking at all, but it calls for not overthinking. When we overthink, our thoughts spiral over situations that we can't change no matter how much we think about them. The reason why so many meditation practices will ask you to still your mind is because your body has more of an impact on your cognition than your thoughts have on your body. Recognizing patterns of overthinking can be humbling. It's about recognizing that there are some things that you can't solve by thinking about them.

SILENCE
EXERCISE

Set a timer for 20 minutes.

Sit in an upright and comfortable position.

Trust the time that you have given to yourself and
the place you have chosen to sit.

Don't worry about whether you might be
more comfortable somewhere else.

Let yourself think about whatever you want.

IMAGINATION
EXERCISE

Go to bed two to three hours earlier than you usually do.

Turn all of your lights off and put on some music if you want to.

✿

Set an intention—maybe you want to come up with the plot for
a story or figure out what love means to you.

✿

Ask your imagination to give you what you asked for.

✿

Let your mind drift without worrying over whether you will get what you asked for.

What are some things that you can't solve by thinking about them?

_____

_____

_____

_____

_____

_____

Are there any things that you are trying to solve this year that are actually lifelong pursuits?

_____

_____

_____

_____

_____

_____

_____

What does moving at your own pace look and feel like?

_____

_____

_____

_____

_____

_____

CHOOSING EASE

A lot of the time, we don't choose the easier way to get to where we want to go. We may just want more of a journey. But sometimes, we have this idea that we will deserve something more if we earn it in the most difficult and self-punishing way possible. We are afraid that we will be punished for enjoying things, so we try to prove to ourselves that we had to suffer for pleasure.

Choosing ease can be about justice. If you choose ease when you can and strengthen those pathways toward it, that can support everybody. Because ability is always temporary, strengthening easiness supports everyone, including those who are not in a position to strive or to do things the hard way. Choosing easiness also can give you more time for other things.

What was a time when you felt as though something was too easy?

_____

_____

_____

_____

_____

When was a time that you were really good at something? When you didn't have to think too hard or try too hard?

_____

_____

_____

_____

_____

_____

What happened before to make it possible for you to find ease? What supported your ease at that moment?

_____

_____

_____

_____

_____

_____

_____

How did you feel about your own ease?

_____

_____

_____

_____

_____

_____

What was a time when you felt that something was too hard?

_____

_____

_____

_____

_____

_____

What did you do in response?

_____

_____

_____

_____

_____

_____

_____

What support could have transformed your difficulty into ease?

_____

_____

_____

_____

_____

_____

_____

_____

How did you feel about your difficulty?

_____

_____

_____

_____

_____

_____

_____

_____

PAYING ATTENTION

Wu wei is not just about letting go of overthinking, of the idea that you can think yourself out of situations. Wu wei is also about paying attention. Jupiter hates overthinking things, but it loves attention.

There's a difference between paranoid attention and nonparanoid attention.

Paranoid attention is when we are overly attached to the idea that observing something ahead of time, being urgent or meticulous, can provoke change. We believe that we can think change into being. Paranoid attention actually diminishes our attention span. When we practice paranoid attention, we are watching out for things that might hurt us or threaten us; we fixate on the things we are most afraid of. For example, you and a friend have the same idea for an essay and you both write the essays. You are upset because you are afraid that the friend will envy you or that you will envy your friend. You begin to avoid the friend.

Attention is not always paranoid, however. With synchronistic attention, you notice the things that are right in front of you and the things that ask for your attention. Synchronistic attention is about noticing the coincidences, or synchronicities, that make wonder possible. It allows your attention to charm you. You notice when you come across a headline or a book that is exactly the thing that you were wondering about last night. You notice that you and the person across from you on the train are both wearing the same shirt, and you strike up a conversation. Synchronistic attention requires that you pay attention. In the example of the friend with the essay, you and your friend have the same idea for an essay and you both write the essays. You recognize that your friend must be responding to similar conditions as you and that there is a new dialogue possible that wasn't there before. You are excited to talk to your friend about the miraculousness of intellectual coincidence.

During your commute, try to pay attention to all of the things that draw your attention. Did you notice that someone had mismatched socks on? Wonder whether someone with a surfboard was coming from the beach? Notice a baby in a stroller staring at you? At the end of your commute, write down everything that you can remember.

- Take a walk around your neighborhood and take a photo of everything that you are noticing for the first time.

- Call attention to coincidences when you notice them. Make a big deal out of them. Ask other people around you to notice them with you. Let them go after you feel satisfied with the attention you have given the coincidence.

- Choose a color, word, or number. Follow that color, word, or number for a week, a month, or a year. Take a picture or write down in a special note-book every instance in which you run into that color, word, or number.

- Stare out a window and let your eye follow whatever it is called to. Do this until you notice repetitions.

- Make a color tree poem. Find some watercolors or acrylic paint, and some paintbrushes. Mix a color, any color. Paint a swatch of this color on the following page. Keep mixing colors and place them in different spots on the page. Once you are satisfied with your colors, make a color tree by drawing lines from paint swatches to other paint swatches. Name these colors whimsically. Journal in the margins about these names.

"Building flow is about giving yourself enough time to stumble into a flow state, about taking away distraction so that you can relax in your flow state, but it is also about doing things that you actually want to do."

BUILDING FLOW BY RECOGNIZING DESIRE

Jupiter, being part water, is a planet that flows. Building flow is about giving yourself enough time to stumble into a flow state, about taking away distraction so that you can relax in your flow state, but it is also about doing things that you actually want to do.

Desire is crucial for flow. If you usually find flow while reading but you're just more interested in science fiction than in anything else this year, then you're not going to find satisfaction flow reading anything but science fiction. If you find flow through conversation and your main topic lately is a dating reality show you've been watching, there might be something about the show's premise that you're interested in, whether that is love, the art of conversation, or a memory of your own love experience.

Directing passion, interest, or desire into a flow requires the use of tools—such as a story, a composition, or a rhythm. If you're interested in the art of conversation, for example, and this appetite shows up through your interest in a dating reality show, you can direct this passion into a creative flow state by using the rhythm of flirting. You might flirt platonically, romantically, or sexually through words or glances or touches. If you're interested in world-building and this passion shows up in your love of science fiction, you can direct this interest by creating your own story. You might write your own story that exposes, and hides, part of a world that you build.

What was the last thing that captured your interest?

_____

_____

_____

_____

_____

What about the thing actually interested you?

_____

_____

_____

_____

_____

What would be the easiest way to give your interest satisfactory attention?

_____

_____

_____

_____

_____

What tools do you have to direct your interest into a state of flow?

_____

_____

_____

_____

_____

_____

♄

SATURN RETURN

FREQUENCY	SIGNIFICANCE	WHEN IT HAPPENS
Occurs approximately every 30 years	Physical changes, boundaries, getting older, mortality, grief	Begins when Saturn returns to the sign of your natal Saturn and ends when Saturn leaves that sign

SATURN RETURNS TEND TO HAPPEN just a few times—when you grow from being a young adult into an actual adult (when you're around 29 or 30), another time when you're around 60 (when you enter elderhood), and then a third time when you transition into becoming an ancestor around age 90.

A lot of the time, people share a Jupiter placement or a Saturn placement with a parent or other family member. If you share Jupiter or Saturn with a parent, you will go through the returns together. You might watch a family member such as a parent become an elder as you become an adult or a child become an adult as you become an elder.

Reflecting on Your Last Saturn Cycle

Saturn returns are about reversals, since Saturn is a planet that is celebrated through reversals. Saturn is known as both a father and a son. As a son, he usurped his father, Uranus. As a father, he was usurped by his son Jupiter. When you go through a return of Saturn, you tend to go through topsy-turvy reversals. You may suddenly realize that you're not as dedicated to things you had thought you'd spend a lifetime on, you realize that you're not as good at certain things that you thought you needed to be perfect at, and you also realize that you have what it takes to get better at things that you assumed you weren't good at.

What were the dates of your last Saturn return? You can consult an ephemeris or count 28 to 30 years back from your current age. Ages when your Saturn returns, loosely, are: 28 to 30, 58 to 60, and 88 to 90. If your natal Saturn is retrograde, your Saturn return might have happened at 30 to 32, 60 to 62, or 90 to 92.

How did being that age change your life? What was life like at that age?

_____

_____

_____

_____

_____

_____

What was your last Saturn opposition like? You would count 15 years after your last Saturn return. Saturn oppositions tend to happen, loosely, around the ages of 15, 45, 75, and 105.

_____

_____

_____

Are there any things that you started during your last Saturn return that reached a culmination point during your last Saturn opposition?

_____

_____

_____

_____

_____

_____

_____

What about the dates of the opening Saturn square in your last Saturn cycle? What was life like the last time you were 7, 37, 67, or 97?

_____

_____

_____

_____

_____

_____

_____

_____

How about the dates of the closing Saturn square in your last Saturn cycle? What was it like being 22, 52, or 82?

_____

_____

_____

_____

_____

_____

_____

Did anything happen during those ages that disturbed the things you began during your last Saturn return?

_____

_____

_____

_____

_____

_____

_____

How do you feel about those things now?

_____

_____

_____

_____

_____

_____

_____

Do you want to bring those things into your next Saturn cycle? How do you want those things to change?

_____

_____

_____

_____

_____

_____

_____

When you were a kid, what did you think being an adult would mean?

_____

_____

_____

_____

_____

_____

_____

How were you taught adulthood? And by whom?

_____

_____

_____

_____

_____

_____

What are some things that you assumed personal guilt for that are actually out of your control?

What is in your control?

What happens when you assume your personal capacity to be larger than it is?

What do you allow for yourself when you no longer assume that you will "get in trouble"?

_____

_____

_____

_____

_____

_____

_____

_____

_____

_____

_____

Write a letter to the adult that you thought you had to be when you were a kid. Thank that person for what they have done for you and tell them that you no longer need them.

_____

_____

_____

_____

_____

_____

_____

_____

_____

_____

_____

Shame

Saturn is a planet that carries shame, so let's talk about it.

Shame sometimes feels red hot. Other times, it feels chilling. It makes us quiet down or it makes us speak so fast that hardly anyone can understand us. It makes us take up more space without deserving it or it makes us leave the rooms that we worked hard to be in. Shame is sometimes impossible to talk about. It's unintelligible because it can feel like a secret that no one is supposed to know.

The *Oxford English Dictionary* defines shame as a consciousness around wrongdoing. The relationship between shame and consciousness is import-ant. We all enact harm every day—when we buy a banana, we are exploiting plantations and workers in the Philippines; when we turn on the gas, we con-tribute to a market for energy extraction and depletion; and when we take out the trash, we contribute to a landfill. However, it is very rare for us to become conscious of the harm that we enact because this takes something remarkable—it takes knowing and caring about someone who we oppress.

If we hold shame that we are meant to carry, we also are sometimes taught to internalize shame that does not belong to us. Racial trauma is often shame that we learn to hold for white oppressors. Children are some-times also shamed for things that are not their own responsibilities. Shame is not just about wrongdoing. It is also a suspicion that you are somehow a wrong person for existing in the way you exist.

There is also survival shame—the shame around having survived some-thing that other people or life forms did not. I call this survival shame and not survival guilt. It turns out, the *Oxford English Dictionary* is a little off.

Shame is not only a feeling about wrongdoing. We feel shame about surviving, we feel shame that isn't our own, and we also feel shame that is true to us and honest to feel.

While some self-help books tell us that shame is inherently an unhealthy emotion (as though any emotion can be inherently unhealthy), we live in a world where we are compelled to do harm, where our choices are often limited to the ones that harm. It would be shocking and catastrophic if we were able to simply get rid of shame. What compounds the difficulty of expressing shame is the exiling of shame. We are told that shame is not healthy, and we are not taught how to metabolize it or express it.

Shame is an important emotion that may need more attention from us than we have been taught to give it. Feeling shame is okay and feeling shame does not mean that you become shame. Shame has an incredible creative potential. Humor, kink, and theater are all places where people of all stripes have come to explore and express shame in privacy and collaboration.

What types of shame have you been carrying for your oppressors?

What does this shame feel like in your body? Does it numb you out? Does it make you close up? Does it make you trust some people less?

_____

_____

_____

_____

_____

_____

_____

_____

_____

What types of shame are you carrying because of your place in society?

_____

_____

_____

_____

_____

_____

_____

_____

_____

_____

What does this shame feel like in your body? Does it feel invasive, like something that makes you turn away from yourself? Does it make you want to hide? You might notice that the shame that you carry for your oppressors feels different from the shame that you are meant to carry as an oppressor.

Because shame is a difficult emotion, it is an emotion that we can get trapped in or fear getting trapped in. *There is a difference between feeling shame and identifying with shame or becoming trapped inside of it.* Sometimes, we are so afraid that we will get trapped in shame that we exile shame as an emotion. Freezing and contempt are two common defenses against shame.

Feeling shame and expressing shame are not the same as getting trapped in shame. In fact, we are more likely to be trapped in shame when we try to get rid of it because we don't know how to feel or express it. Accepting and loving the parts of you that are responsible for shame is liberating. Shame is a powerful emotion. Teaching yourself how to move into and then out of shame can be empowering, creative, and loving. When you listen to shame and encourage it to come out from a trapped place, you allow it to grow and mature with you.

GETTING CURIOUS ABOUT SHAME

What defends you against shame?

Do your defenses against shame need anything from you before they allow you to explore the shame that they protect you against? (People tend to explore shame in privacy because shame is so often threatened by exposure.)

What is your shame trying to do for you?

_____

_____

_____

_____

_____

_____

What does your shame need from you?

_____

_____

_____

_____

_____

_____

_____

How do you know when shame has overwhelmed you?

_____

_____

_____

_____

_____

_____

_____

What can support you when easing out of shame?

_____

_____

_____

_____

_____

_____

_____

_____

_____

_____

What might make it feel important to you to return to shame so that you can explore it more? Is there anything that you are curious about? What would you like to ask shame?

_____

_____

_____

_____

_____

_____

_____

_____

_____

_____

_____

Making an Accountability-Ask

It's not easy asking for accountability. Very often, we find it easier to normalize harm, make excuses, and gloss over things rather than making our relationships more accountable and more intimate. We ask ourselves why we have chosen to "make a big deal" about a particular instance over all of the other times we were harmed.

When we ask a person or a group of people for accountability for how they have hurt us, it is not related to the magnitude of the harm. It is related to closeness. We ask for accountability for harm when we choose to be close with someone or when we are forced to be close to them. Sometimes, we ask friends who hurt us to be accountable for that hurt because we love them and want to continue being friends with them. At times, we might ask for accountability from a workplace that has harmed us because we do not have the option of leaving that job.

Asking for accountability is terrifying. It is terrifying in the same way that verbalizing attachment or asserting a need is terrifying. When we ask someone for accountability we are telling them, "I need you to do something for me." There is always the possibility of rejection. Asking for accountability is about showing a need for a relationship to become closer. It is terrifying for all of the same reasons that attaching to someone is terrifying.

Asking for accountability from a workplace or other place that you do not necessarily desire a relationship with but are forced to be in relationship with can be frustrating. It is frustrating to have to put in the work to bring more closeness in a relationship that you do not choose, especially when you do not feel safe enough making an accountability-ask in the first place.

ACCOUNTABILITY IS ATTACHMENT

When you decide whether or not you want to make an accountability-ask, ask yourself whether you plan to stay in relationship with the person or people you are asking for accountability from and not about the validity of your pain. Your need for accountability is not the same as your need for emotional validation. It is possible to validate harm without pursuing a relationship with the person who harmed you if you do not choose to continue a relationship with that person. Asking for accountability means that you are asking for a more sincere and vulnerable attachment.

Do you choose to continue to be in relationship with the person or people who have caused you harm?

_____

_____

_____

_____

If you choose to be in relationship with the person or people who have harmed you, what needs to happen in that relationship before you feel like the harm is acknowledged adequately?

_____

_____

_____

_____

What needs to happen before you feel safe in that relationship?

_____

_____

_____

_____

If you choose to no longer be in relationship with the person or people who have harmed you, what will help you understand your pain outside of that relationship?

_____

_____

_____

_____

What are some things that will help you metabolize the loss of that attachment?

_____

_____

_____

_____

_____

_____

_____

COMMUNICATING THE ASK

How might you communicate your needs in an accountability-ask? Imagine yourself communicating your ask, whether that is in person, through email, or on the phone. What emotions come to the forefront when you imagine yourself asking for accountability? Circle any that apply or add your own.

Anger	Fear	Surprise
Anxiety	Insecurity	Tiredness
Calm	Joy	Triumph
Closeness	Numbness	_____
Comfort	Openheartedness	_____
Confidence	Pride	_____
Exhaustion	Shame	_____

How might you support any of the emotions that come up
when you make an accountability-ask?

EXAMPLES OF HOW YOU MIGHT SUPPORT YOURSELF

- Phone call with a friend before or after the conversation
- Attention from someone who was there at the conversation
- Attention from someone who wasn't there at the conversation

- Quiet time alone
- Heavy blankets
- Touch
- Time off
- Sleep
- Travel

FACILITATING CONVERSATIONS ON HARM

Facilitating a conflict can be a beautiful experience. Remember—when someone asks for accountability from someone else instead of sweeping the problem under a rug, they are asking for a more durable attachment. They are asking for more love. When you are asked to facilitate conflict, you are being asked to support a relationship between two people.

When you are asked to facilitate a conflict, you may wonder: Am I the right person to do this? Journal on the following questions to work this out.

What might your presence bring up for each person involved in the conflict?

_____

_____

_____

_____

Do you have any history with either person or will your presence make anyone less likely to trust a facilitation space?

_____

_____

_____

_____

What are the goals of the facilitation? What would an end to the facilitation process, if not the conflict, look like?

_____

_____

_____

_____

What would it take you, as a facilitator, to bring the room toward these goals?

_____

_____

_____

_____

_____

Do you honestly have the capacity, resources, and time to bring the group closer to its goals?

_____

_____

_____

_____

_____

Do you believe that the relationship you are being asked to support is an ethical one?

_____

_____

_____

_____

_____

What would make you need to drop out of facilitating the conflict?

_____

_____

_____

_____

_____

PREPARING FOR FACILITATION

Before you bring people together, reflect on these questions:

- Is everyone involved in the conflict supported adequately outside of the conflict space? Is there any unevenness? Is the person harmed less supported or resourced than the person who caused harm, or vice versa?
- How close are you to the events that led to the conflict? Are there any details of what happened that you need to know in order to move the group closer to its goals? Are there any details that you do not need to know to move the group closer to its goals?
- How much time needs to go by before the conflict can be addressed? What needs to happen before everyone is supported enough to understand what happened?

Make a list of conditions that need to be met before you facilitate a conversation. Ask everyone involved, including the person who was harmed, the person who harmed, and anyone else who might show up for the conversation, to do the same.

EXAMPLES OF WHAT CONDITIONS MIGHT LOOK LIKE

- Both people involved in the conflict, the harmed and the person who did the harm, must have access to stable housing and time before you sit down and talk.
- You do not want to know what happened, since the goal is to decide how to share community spaces.
- You need to know what happened, since the goal is to acknowledge harm.

- This reminds you of a past instance where you were harmed. You need support in understanding that past instance of harm before you can facilitate this conflict.
- You need clearly agreed-upon rules about when people get to talk during the facilitated conversation.

Supporting
Your Past, Present,
and Future

Saturn returns always take away the things that weigh you down, even if you're very attached to those things. It's humility, which is not just about taking apart your ego but also about remembering that your limits are not more real than your dreams. Saturn returns are about remembering that the future is unplannable and uncertain. Saturn returns are about believing in possibility.

Use the map on the next page to make a list of needs. List your own individual needs, the needs that you have in your relationships, the needs that you share with the communities that you are involved with, and the needs that you share with your society in a broad sense. Fill this map out as many times as you like.

When you complete this diagram, write in needs that you are already meeting in addition to needs that you crave. Do some dreaming. What needs do you dream about being able to fill? Get as specific as possible.

EXAMPLES OF NEEDS

- I need to be able to rely on consistent care for my illness.
- We need expansive mutual aid that doesn't only respond to crisis.
- My cat needs to be fed every day.
- My child needs neighborhood friends.
- I need three hours to write every day.

- I need to be left alone when I am in the bathroom.
- I need stable housing.
- I need an accountability system to address my alcoholism.
- We need more gardens and fewer parking lots.

SOCIETAL:
What needs do you share with an
entire society that you participate in?

COMMUNAL:
What needs do you share with
your larger communities?

RELATIONAL:
What needs do you share
with people you know?

PERSONAL:
What needs do you have
as one person?

Once you have your list of needs, assess them honestly. Figure out how much time, capacity, and resources each need takes to fill. Be honest with yourself about how much it takes for each need to truly feel full.

Honesty around capacity is difficult because we undervalue ourselves. We often think "soft skills" like listening or compassion take less time to cultivate. For example, a need like "I need to feel heard" or "My friend needs to be listened to" can seem like it doesn't take a lot to fill when, in reality, the type of listening that is needed is a skill that can take years to cultivate.

For each need you listed, consider the following:

What kind of time does it take to fill this need?
- Can you measure the time you need adequately?
- Do you need a shift in attention or consistent time?

What resources does it take to fill this need?
- Can you measure the resources you need adequately?

What capacity does it take to fill this need?
- How much capacity would make it possible for you to respond to this need enthusiastically?

What does, or would, trusting the filling of this need give you in terms of time, resources, and capacity?

After assessing your needs, put them into categories. The categories are as follows on the facing page.

NEEDS THAT I AM ALREADY FILLING WITH SATISFACTION

NEEDS THAT I AM STRUGGLING TO FILL

NEEDS THAT I DREAM OF SEEING FILLED

Take a look at your list. Now move the needs in the first category above into the first category below. Then move the needs that you listed out of the second and third categories and into the other categories in your timeline of needs.

Needs that you are already filling with satisfaction:

_____

_____

_____

Needs that you can begin to meet with satisfaction within one week:

_____

_____

_____

Needs that you can begin to meet with satisfaction within three months:

_____

_____

_____

Needs that you can plan to see filled in one year:

_____

_____

_____

Needs that you dream about seeing filled in five years:

_____

_____

_____

Needs that you dream about seeing filled in ten years:

_____

_____

_____

Needs that you dream about seeing filled in fifty years:

_____

_____

_____

REFLECTING
ON THE EXERCISE

Put a 1 next to each personal need in your timeline of needs that you just created, a 2 next to every relational need, a 3 next to every communal need, and a 4 next to every societal need. Do you notice any patterns? What do you notice?

Look back to how you assessed each need. Next to the needs listed in your timeline, pencil in the different types of support connected to each need.

Celebrate the needs that you are meeting in a satisfactory way. Celebrating your filled needs can look like accepting compliments about the wellness you experience as a result of fulfilled needs, being outspoken about how good it feels for needs to be met, and about paying forward the benefits that you receive from having your needs be met.

Keep your list of needs nearby and add to it whenever you want.

ALICE SPARKLY KAT is an astrologer. They use astrology to re-chart a history of the subconscious, redefine the body in world, and reimagine history as collective memory. Their astrological work has inhabited the Museum of Modern Art in New York, the Philadelphia Museum of Art, and the Brooklyn Museum. They're also the author of *Postcolonial Astrology*.

THIS BOOK IS DEDICATED TO Yoongi-bear, the sweetest calico cat to ever grace the streets of Bushwick, with the bushiest tail and the softest paws. You chose me and I chose you. I live my life for you now and you are well aware of it.

ISBN 978-1-7972-2223-3

Manufactured in China.

Design by Kelley Galbreath.
Typesetting by Kelley Galbreath. Typeset in Freight Sans.

10 9 8 7 6 5 4 3 2 1

This book contains advice and information relating to health and interpersonal well-being. It is not intended to replace medical or psychotherapeutic advice and should be used to supplement rather than replace any needed care by your doctor or mental health professional. While all efforts have been made to ensure accuracy of the information contained in this book as of date of publication, the publisher and the author are not responsible for any adverse effects or consequences that may occur as a result of applying the methods suggested in this book.

Chronicle books and gifts are available at special quantity discounts to corporations, professional associations, literacy programs, and other organizations. For details and discount information, please contact our premiums department at corporatesales@chroniclebooks.com or at 1-800-759-0190.

 CHRONICLE PRISM

Chronicle Prism is an imprint of Chronicle Books LLC, 680 Second Street, San Francisco, California 94107

www.chronicleprism.com